Women Learning To Shoot

A Guide for Law Enforcement Officers

Diane Nicholl & Vicki Farnam

Women Learning To Shoot:
A Guide for Law Enforcement Officers
by Diane Nicholl & Vicki Farnam

© 2006 by DTI Publications, Inc
All rights reserved.

Printed in the United States of America. No part of this book may be used or reproduced in any form or by any means, or stored in a database or retrieval system, without prior written permission of the publisher, except in the case of brief quotations embodied in critical articles and reviews. Making copies of any part of this book for any purpose other than your own personal use is a violation of United States copyright laws.

For information, address:
DTI Publications, Inc.
PO Box 18746
Boulder, CO 80308-1746

ISBN-13: 978-0-9659422-6-3
ISBN-10: 0-9659422-6-0

Cover photo by Kirk Webb
Cover design by Shasti O'Leary Soudant, www.shasti.com

Warning and Disclaimer

This book is sold as is, without warranty of any kind, either expressed or implied. While every precaution has been taken in the preparation of this book, the author and DTI Publications, Inc. assume no responsibility for errors or omissions. Neither the author nor DTI Publications, Inc. shall have any liability to any person or entity with respect to any loss or damage caused or alleged to be caused directly or indirectly by the instructions contained in this book. It is further stated that neither the author nor DTI Publications, Inc. assumes any responsibility for the use or misuse of the information or instructions contained herein.

To our students, past, present and future

About the Authors

Diane Nicholl grew up where guns were commonplace. She has enjoyed shooting from the time she was ten years old and would go plinking with a 22 single shot rifle. She worked in the field of neurophysiology for 15 years before finding she could no longer balance research and teaching firearms classes. In 1996, she started her own business, DTI Publications, Inc., where she teaches firearms courses and publishes firearms training books. She is a Colorado POST certified law enforcement firearms instructor and an NRA Training Counselor.

Vicki Farnam has been teaching firearms with her husband, John Farnam, of Defense Training International, Inc. since 1986. They travel all across the country. She has taught defensive shooting classes for women only and classes for instructors about teaching women. Those classes have been for non-law enforcement as well as law enforcement on local, state and federal levels.

Diane and Vicki welcome your comments or questions. Please contact them at www.DTIPubs.com.

Cover photo shows Capt. Rebecca Spiess and Lt. Laurie Galvan of the Mesa County Sheriff's Office performing an exercise that separates sight alignment and trigger manipulation.

Acknowledgments

It is with sincere appreciation that I thank many friends, colleagues and associates for their part in continuing my education, for their help in assisting with classes for women and their continuing support of students seeking to improve their skills. To John, Diane and Kirk, Kris Peterson, Wendi Lankister, and Steve Hoch, a special thanks for all of their encouragement and hard work and for keeping me focused. The following is a list of all the others whose work and dedication have a part in this book. John Adler, Colby Adler, Ann Berry, Shawn Bjerke, Keith Brown, SuAnn Cook, Gordon Cook, Andy Evans, Kate Camp, Steve Camp, Scott Camp, Pauline Farnam, Phil Farnam, Wes Garner, Jeff Chudwin, Dennis Tueller, Jen and John Coy, Sue Garthwaite, Susie Gochenour, Scott Coffee, Marc Dalhsten, Steve Van Mol, Joe Smolarz, Neil Mathews, Gregg Garrett, Michelle Garrett, Tom Burris, Jerry Hollombe, Lydia Uribe, Paula Bratich, Frank Sharpe, Angelo Novelli, Kathy Batterman, Larry Nichols, Dave Manning, Marcus Ward, Pete Tausig, Toni Camp, Frank Pytko, Jack Richards, Richard Green, Marc Richard, Jack Branson, Jeff Donnell, Deb Donnell, Vivian Crowder, Billy Stowers, Mike Bradford, Manny Kapelsohn, Lou Alessi, Pete Pi, Elaine Pi, Lockie Sailer, Dennis Tobin, Daryl Smith, Andy LouDerBack, Stan Heckrodt, Wes Heckrodt, Bill Hollar, Rob Sikora, Linda Zerwin, Rocky Mountain Women in Law Enforcement and the International Association of Law Enforcement Firearms Instructors.

And thanks to those who fight daily for us, Lt. Colonel Freddie Blish, Captain Madeline Melendez, Chief Warrant Officer Phil Ross, Master Sergeant Earl Mitchell, Master Sergeant Mark Godfrey, all of the rest of the men and women of the United States Marine Corps with whom we have worked, and those in the United States Army, Navy and Air Force.

Thanks to Capt. Rebecca Spiess and Lt. Laurie Galvan of the Mesa County Sheriff's Office for their excellent examples of competent shooters.

Vicki and I spent many days writing at the Lakeside Inn on Lake Tahoe. I appreciate the wonderful hospitality and tranquil environment. Kirk Webb did an outstanding job of keeping me sane and getting this book to press. We could not have done it without him. Thanks to Ann Berry, Earl Perry and Frank Pytko for help with the proofs. A special thanks to Karen Melcher for her patience in helping with the photographs. John and Jenny Higgs and Robb Ray were always ready to provide support. To all the women I have taught and who shoot with me; I have learned from each of you. Thanks to Scott Little for sharing his knowledge of law enforcement and instructing. Thank you to John Farnam for his encouragement and support.

Even though she has told me time and again, "I will never write another book!" I want to thank Vicki for the untold hours of collaboration that made our second book possible.

Contents

Chapter 1. Risk and Opportunity — 1
Chapter 2. Stance — 5
Chapter 3. Grip — 17
Chapter 4. Sight Alignment — 29
Chapter 5. Trigger Control — 41
Chapter 6. Launch Platform — 55
Chapter 7. Recoil — 63
Chapter 8. Safety — 71
Appendix. Gunhandling Skills — 81
Glossary — 107
Index — 123
Resources — 127

Introduction

From Diane

Women Learning To Shoot: A Guide for Law Enforcement Officers will help you learn how to hit where you are aiming. We could have written a 600-page encyclopedia on this subject (and I was well on my way to doing that) but we realized there are many resource books about handgun shooting. Our book is different because it is written for women by women.

We have listened, asked questions and observed how women learn to shoot for many years. Our students include women shooting a handgun for the first time to those with many years experience in law enforcement and the military. They share many of the same problems and frustrations, so do not feel like you are the only one struggling to hit the target!

At the beginning of every class, we ask our students what their shooting problems are. The most frequent complaint is their lack of consistency. Sometimes they go to the range and shoot well and other times they do poorly. They can not explain why this happens.

This means they do not fully understand what they need to do to accurately hit their target and they do not know why they miss. Our book provides the information you need to learn to make consistently accurate hits and to be able to self correct if you miss.

There are many things that can help or hinder accurate shooting. You will find that shooting requires you to do several things all at the same time. We break shooting down into parts, thoroughly explain each one and describe how to put them together.

From Vicki

Ever since Diane and I have been teaching male law enforcement firearms instructors about teaching women how to shoot, and when we wrote *Teaching Women To Shoot, A Law Enforcement Instructors's Guide*, we have been reminding them that most women need more details and more time to absorb that detail than the average male the instructors teach. Time is a precious and costly commodity however, and not all instructors can find more of it. One suggestion we have made to solve this problem is to provide written material for the female student to review away from the range or classroom.

This book is the answer to that dilemma. The following chapters are filled with minutiae that you can read and reread if you need more time and detail to understand the fundamentals of learning to shoot accurately. It can be used for study and review if you are a student in an academy setting when you have extra time beyond the constraints of the formal classroom or range sessions. It will help the academy instructor expand his or her limited amount of time available for instructing.

This book will also be useful if you are a working officer struggling with firearms qualifications. We have lost count of the number of female officers we have encountered in our classes who have told us that no one has ever explained sight picture and sight alignment to them in the 1, 3, 8 or even 15 years they have been law enforcement officers. Of course that is not what their instructors would say, but whatever *was* taught didn't make sense or wasn't understood completely, and they don't ask for clarification. Here now is your review to read and study to improve your understanding of the fundamentals of accurate shooting.

The final responsibility falls to you. Learning to shoot accurately is to your benefit. Be victorious!

The machine and operator

A handgun is only a machine. It is designed to do one thing – launch a bullet in the direction of an intended target. To do this the trigger is pressed all the way to rear. This releases the hammer or striker that hits the firing pin. The firing pin hits the primer in the cartridge, causing the powder in the cartridge to burn. The burning powder creates the force used to push the bullet out of the cartridge, down the barrel and on its path (trajectory) to the target. The gun has now fired.

Should you need to fire your gun, your job (as the operator) is to hold the gun steady, aim it and press the trigger so the bullet hits the intended target. You are the "Launch Platform."

Driving a car is also an interaction with a mechanical device. As driver, you have to be able to perform several tasks at the same time. You have to watch the road and be ready to respond to unexpected events while you drive to your destination. You learn to drive because you want to and are motivated by the freedom and independence driving gives you.

Shooting a handgun also involves performing several tasks at the same time, however it is no more complex than driving. You may learn to shoot a handgun because you want to or you may do it because it is a requirement of your job. We hope you are motivated to learn to shoot accurately because it is a skill that can save your life or the lives of those you protect.

Chapter 1

Risk and Opportunity

Learning to shoot a handgun takes you out of your comfort zone. It involves both physical and mental risk. The physical risk of shooting is that you can be seriously injured or you could seriously injure someone else if you do not handle your gun properly. You may have to use your gun to protect yourself and that may involve injury or death for someone else. If you cannot handle your gun with skill when you need to use it to defend yourself, you may be seriously injured or even killed.

The mental risk involved with learning to shoot is the embarrassment and frustration of not being able to pass your qualification.

You can manage the physical risk by learning and practicing safe gunhandling skills. At first you may feel awkward, uncertain, or even scared but these feelings will diminish as you practice. In time you will understand how your gun works and how to handle it safely. An instructor or range officer will guide you as you learn, but you are responsible for learning gunhandling skills. You are the one who controls how you interact with the gun in your hand.

You learn by doing, not just watching, listening or reading. The only way to become comfortable handling your gun is to practice. With practice, you will discover how well you can perform each skill. Each success builds your confidence.

Managing the mental risk involved in shooting is hard work. You have to train yourself to stay mentally focused and concentrate on what your body (hands, arms, shoulders, torso) must do to make an accurate shot. It is easy to become distracted and let your body go on autopilot, overruling what your mind knows is correct procedure. Unless you have practiced well and developed good muscle memory, your body may react physically in anticipation of recoil, moving the front sight and causing you to miss.

You will encounter many speed bumps such as lack of information, guns that are too big or too small, recoil that is punishing, rainy days, poor instruction, headaches or stomach aches. These are things that clutter your mind. Do not use them as excuses for why you miss the target! Stay focused, keep the clutter out of your mind and you can do it!

Invest in yourself. You can decide what the risk will bring you; the opportunity to succeed or to fail. The choice is yours.

Qualification

It is your responsibility to learn how to hit the target accurately. During qualifications, you are required to fire a number of accurate shots in a given period of time. If you miss too many, you fail. If you take too long, you fail. Get the clutter out of your mind and focus on what it takes to make an accurate hit.

Qualifications are hard! Knowing that a qualification is coming up can make you feel nervous, apprehensive or even sick to your stomach. Your thoughts may be filled with the same phrase repeating over and over in your mind, "What if I fail? What if I fail?"

Why do we tend to say "What if I fail?" instead of "I'm going to succeed, I'm going to succeed!" It's easy for your mind to get stuck with "I'm going to fail." Sometimes we can fool ourselves into thinking that everyone, including ourselves, is expecting us to fail, so it is actually easier to face the failure than face the success. If you failed once in the past, your mind thinks it is logical you will fail again. It is easy to get used to failure. In a way, it is more comfortable to fail.

Success can be scary! If you succeed, then there will be an expectation from others that you will *always* succeed and that adds a great deal of pressure! Someone else may make fun of you if you succeed. They might ask you what took you so long to figure it out. You might even shoot better than someone else. They might think you are showing off. So what! You must not let negative thoughts about the consequences of success hinder you from doing your best. Success is risky but gives you the opportunity to have confidence in yourself!

Shooting faster or from longer distances

The risk in learning to shoot faster is that you will miss even more. Accept that you will have misses as you push yourself. Accuracy comes first, speed will follow. Stay focused in the present moment. If you are thinking about the shot you missed, you may not notice what your body is doing when you press the trigger for your next shot. There is nothing you can do about the miss, just let

Chapter 1: Risk and Opportunity

it go. Don't punish yourself when you miss. Self punishment gets in the way of success.

Shooting from longer distances during a qualification is similar. Remind yourself to align the sights and continue to align the sights while you press the trigger smoothly. Stay focused on the challenge of hitting at 15 or even 25 yards. Focus on the front sight. Stop thinking of how many misses you have had in the past.

Fear of success

You may worry that if you shoot well once, it will be expected of you every time you go to the range. You may doubt your ability to repeat your performance in three or six months. You might think "what if it is only because I managed to hold it together once, but the pressure of repeating the success is overwhelming and I will fail."

If you continue to fear success, you will certainly bring on failure. Know what you have to do, be prepared and be well satisfied with yourself when you succeed.

It would be nice if we could "wish" ourselves to success. Instead, we have to step up and take the risk that brings us opportunity. If you are willing to take the risk and you have studied and practiced the skills you need, you will give yourself the opportunity for success, competence and confidence! No one else can do it for you.

Chapter 2

Stance

Stance refers to how you decide to position your feet, legs, hips, torso, shoulders and arms when you prepare to draw your handgun from the holster, bring the gun to eye level, fire and recover from recoil. You can have these body parts in a variety of different positions, but choosing how to arrange yourself to create a good stance and then doing it the same way every time will provide you the most benefit.

- A good stance helps you maintain your balance and stability when drawing your gun and bringing it to eye level.
- A good stance helps you consistently bring your gun to the same place in front of your dominant eye, making it easier to find and align the sights.
- A good stance helps you maintain your balance while you absorb the recoil and then return the gun to eye level.
- A good stance helps you re-acquire the sights and then realign them with the target.
- A good stance improves accuracy by helping you keep your sight alignment as steady as possible while you press the trigger.
- A good stance provides the support you need to keep your gun at eye level as long as necessary.
- A good stance helps you act as the "Launch Platform" (see chapter 6.)
- A good stance will bring your gun in front of your eye even in low light conditions.

As with anything else, practice the ideal, but if circumstances prevent you from being in an "ideal" stance, do not let that be an excuse to fail. Do the best you can to be successful.

> **Tip**
> You can practice your stance without having a gun in your hand.

The most common stances are the Weaver and isosceles. One or the other will work well for most shooters. Either can be modified to fit your physical requirements. The important thing is to find what works best for you and then use it consistently.

If you are right handed, your right hand is the strong side and your left hand is the support side. If you are left handed, your left hand is the strong side and your right hand is the support side. We will use the terms strong and support for now. Remember what these terms mean for your body.

Weaver stance

The Weaver stance works well because of where it positions the gun in relation to the upper body. The weight of the gun is kept close to the upper body with the arms bent.

Muscle fatigue in the arms, shoulders and lower back develops more slowly than when the gun is held away from the body as it is in the isosceles stance. Bending your elbows will help absorb recoil. As a tactical issue, you become a smaller target when using the Weaver stance, though you may expose your side to injury if you wear body armor that does not wrap all the way around your body.

Getting into the Weaver stance

The following directions are for a right handed shooter. Left hand directions follow.

Body position

Facing in the direction of the target, stand with your feet about shoulder-width apart.

Now, pick up your strong side foot and keeping your strong-side hip and shoulder

Chapter 2: Stance

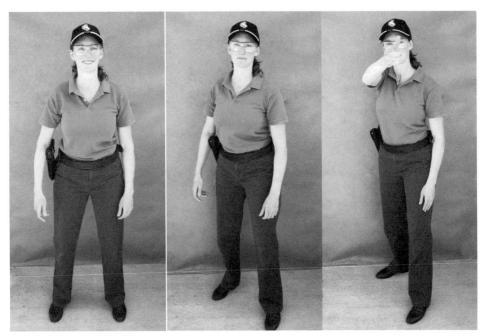

in line with your foot, rotate the strong side of your body away from the target by about 45 degrees. Make sure your strong side hip is over your strong side foot and your strong side shoulder is over your strong side hip. Your chest will rotate about 45 degrees making your support side shoulder further forward than your strong side shoulder. Your head and eyes stay facing downrange at the target. Your chest is at a 45 degree angle. You do not want your chest and shoulders square to the target because you lose the shock absorbing benefits of the stance.

Your knees should be slightly flexed. Keep your back straight and your shoulders relaxed.

Balance

If you stand with your feet shoulder-width apart and your weight evenly distributed on both feet, you create a stable platform for yourself. When your feet are together, your body can sway in any direction or be pushed off balance by recoil, forcing you to take a step to regain your balance. The idea is to keep your body balanced and upright rather than leaning on one foot or the other or placing more weight on either your toes or heels. Stay relaxed and avoid locking your knees.

Gun position

When you bring your gun up to eye level with your good two-handed grip (see chapter 3) and your finger in the register position, your strong side has already been rotated away from the target at a 45 degree angle. It is impossible to push your arms straight out toward the target because your right shoulder is farther back than your left. Your right arm is bent slightly at the elbow and the elbow is pointed outward. Your left arm is bent to almost 90 degrees, but the elbow should be rotated so it points at the ground, not out to the side like your right elbow.

When your support elbow is pointed down, the downward pressure will balance the upward pressure on your strong hand produced by recoil. If your support elbow points to the side, the balancing effect is lost. Keep your strong elbow slightly bent so it acts as a shock absorber as the recoil energy moves up your arm to your shoulder.

Hold the gun in both hands with your good two-handed grip. If it feels comfortable to you, you can create isometric tension with your hands and arms to steady the gun. Your strong hand and arm push forward toward the target. Your support hand pulls your strong hand toward your right shoulder. Both elbows should maintain their bent positions.

The isometric pressure of one hand pushing forward and the other pulling back

Chapter 2: Stance

helps to stabilize your grip and the gun. You do not have to hang on for dear life, but have a firm grip. You will feel some tension in your hands, arms and shoulders, but try not to make it any more than necessary. Isometric tension is not required, but some find it useful.

Whenever you use the Weaver stance, be sure you stand up straight, and keep your head up – not tilted to either side. Try not to lean forward or backward from your waist. Either can cause you to be less stable than you would be if you keep your back straight. Leaning forward puts more weight on your toes while leaning back put your weight on your heels. Your body sometimes takes over and you are inclined to lean backward when you are holding something heavy out in front of you. This is your body trying to reestablish its center of gravity. Remind yourself to stay standing straight to stay balanced. Keep your shoulders over your hips, and your hips over your feet. Do not allow your strong shoulder to rotate forward.

Benefits of the Weaver stance

The Weaver stance puts your body at a 45 degree angle to the gun and helps to stabilize your entire body for the jolt of recoil. The angle of the strong side and the bent elbows also help support the weight of the gun because it is closer to the body.

The angle of the strong side and the bent elbows also brings the gun in closer to the body to help support the weight of the gun.

The isosceles stance

This stance is straight forward and easy to assume.

Body position

Facing downrange, stand with your feet about shoulder-width apart and your knees slightly bent. Position your hips over your feet. Keep you head and back straight. Your shoulders are relaxed. Do not lean forward or backward from the waist.

Gun position

Using your good two-handed grip, with your finger in the register position, bring your gun to eye level. Extend both arms straight forward from the shoulder. Avoid locking your elbows. Point your elbows slightly outward. This helps absorb recoil by allowing your arms to move backwards and forwards with the recoil energy. Keep the sights at eye level, your head straight and your shoulders relaxed.

Benefit

Some people like having their gun at arm's length from their eye. They say it allows for a more precise sight picture. The rear sight appears smaller and the front sight is more closely framed by the rear sight than when the gun is held closer to the eye as in the Weaver stance. Also the arms are the same length because the shoulders are kept square to the target.

Potential problem

The weight of the gun is difficult to support in the isosceles stance because it is far from the body at the end of your arms. Your arms, shoulders and lower back tend to tire quickly, and it becomes difficult to keep your arms and the gun steady with all of that weight hanging off the very end with no other support.

Chapter 2: Stance

Also the recoil comes straight back through your arms to your shoulders and can push your weight back on your heels, unbalancing you.

Try both positions. Which stance helps you handle the weight of your gun with the greatest ease and less stress to your lower back?

Impediments to each stance

Depending on the size of your breasts or if you are wearing a ballistic vest, either stance can feel cumbersome. The best way to maintain a good stance is to keep your arms at shoulder height. In this position they are above your breasts or the bulky curve of the armhole of the vest. Try not to tuck your elbows in close to your body.

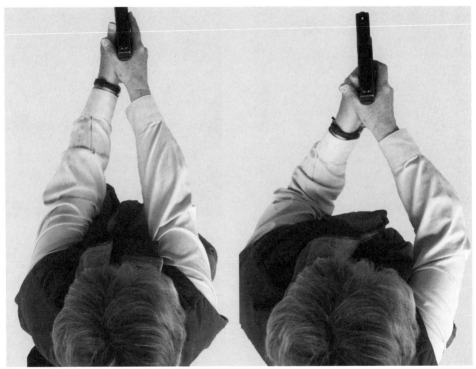

Strength issues

Your lower back takes most of the stress when holding a weight extended in front your body. The Weaver stance may be easier for you because it brings the gun closer to the body. This allows you to hold your gun at eye level for longer periods of time. We encourage you to work to strengthen your upper body and lower back muscles.

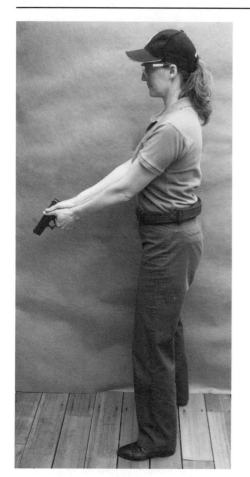 

Take the stress out

If you become fatigued, go to the low ready position. This position allows your arm, shoulder and back muscles a chance to relax momentarily. In either the Weaver or isosceles stance, drop your arms from eye level and point the muzzle at the ground at a 45 degree angle. The muzzle should be pointed about 10 to 12 feet in front of you. Keep your elbow and wrist angles the same as when the gun is at eye level. Be sure your finger is in the register position and your gun is in the appropriate condition for your model of gun, e.g. decocked, safety on. The low ready stance provides relief to your muscles while allowing you to quickly come up to eye level and fire if necessary.

It is easy to lose your mental focus if you are struggling to keep your gun at eye level.

When you are tired, you tend to jerk the trigger in an attempt to get the shooting drill or exercise over with as quickly as possible so you can lower the gun.

Chapter 2: Stance

Leaning back is a common mistake to counterbalance a heavy gun at arms length.

This can occur using either stance if you must hold your gun at eye level for a long time. Bending backward is more prevalent with the isosceles stance, because the gun is held at arm's length. The Weaver stance helps avoid this as the gun is held closer to the body, but some women may still lean back.

> In general, women do not have great upper body strength and tire more quickly when holding a gun at arm's length because the weight is at the end of outstretched arm muscles. Your accuracy may diminish as you become fatigued and your stance deteriorates. You may find yourself leaning back from your waist as you try to counter-balance the weight of the gun.

> **Technical Tip**
>
> Handguns vary in weight from revolvers made of lightweight titanium to high-capacity steel-framed autoloaders. A person with less upper body strength will be able to hold a polymer frame 9mm such as a Glock 19 on target for a longer period of time than they would a full size steel-frame 1911 in 45ACP. As usual, there are trade-offs. While a small lightweight handgun is easier to hold at eye level, the recoil is more pronounced.

The following directions are for a left-handed person

Getting into the Weaver stance

Facing in a safe direction, stand with your feet about shoulder-width apart. Rotate back with your strong side (left) foot from the center line. Just take a small step backward. Your chest rotates about 45 degrees and your right shoulder is forward. Avoid twisting from the waist in an attempt to keep your chest square to the target. Make sure your strong side (left) foot, leg, hip, torso and shoulder are at a 45 degree angle to where they started.

Your head and eyes stay facing downrange at the target. Your chest is at a 45 degree angle. Your strong shoulder is over your strong hip. Your strong hip is over your leg and foot. Your strong foot is at about a 45 degree angle to your support foot. Your feet should still be about shoulder-width apart.

Keep your knees slightly flexed, your back straight and your shoulders relaxed.

Gun position of the Weaver stance, left handed

Using a proper grip, with your trigger finger in the register position, bring your gun to eye level. Without rotating your chest, extend your strong arm (left arm), pointing it at the target until it almost locks.

Your strong hand pushes forward toward the target with the elbow slightly bent. Wrap your support hand (right hand) around your strong hand with both thumbs up. Your support hand pulls your strong hand toward your left shoulder. Your left elbow is slightly bent. Bend your right elbow and rotate it until it points toward the ground.

Your support (right) hand pulls back toward your body with the right elbow

Chapter 2: Stance

bent and pointed toward the ground. When your support elbow points down, the downward pressure will balance the upward pressure on your strong hand that is produced by the weapon's recoil when it fires. If your support elbow points to the side, the balancing effect is lost. Keep your strong (left) elbow slightly bent, so it acts as a shock absorber.

This isometric pressure of one hand pushing forward and the other pulling back helps to stabilize your grip and the gun. You do not have to hang on for dear life, but have a firm grip. You will feel some tension in your hands, arms and shoulders.

Keep your shoulders over your hips. Do not allow your strong shoulder to rotate forward.

Stand straight, keep your head held up – not tilted to either side. The sights should be directly in front of your dominant eye.

Chapter 3

Grip

When it comes to handguns, "grip" has two meanings. The first defines a physical part of a handgun (the handle). The second defines how you place your hands on the gun.

A good grip helps you control your handgun. Placing your hands in a supportive, well defined, consistent grip optimizes your ability to hold the gun, align the sights, control the trigger and control the gun through recoil. A proper grip is not a guarantee of accuracy, but is an integral part of the process.

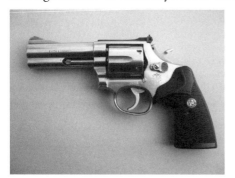 

The grip of the gun

The grip of the gun is the handle you hold. The grip on an autoloader is rectangular and surrounds the magazine well, which contains the magazine. A revolver grip is slightly curved and only serves as a handle.

Either type of grip is part of the frame and has grip covers attached on each side with screws.

Grip covers can be changed to make a better fit for your hand. Grip covers are available in many different materials, but the most common are metal, wood, rubber, plastic or some other synthetic.

The size of the grip of the gun, with covers attached, determines the configuration of "your grip *on* the gun." In other words, the size of the grip determines where your hand and fingers are placed on the grip and how well you can control the gun and reach the various working parts.

Your grip on the gun

Your grip on the gun is the way you wrap your hands and fingers around the grip of your handgun in order to control it. The term grip is used to define a physical part of a handgun and it is also used to define how you place your hands on your gun.

Your grip on the gun allows you to:

- Hold and support the gun
- Align the sights
- Reach the trigger
- Get the leverage you need to press the trigger while holding the sights in alignment
- Control the gun during recoil
- Regain your sight picture after recoil
- Retain control of the gun should someone try to take it from you.

Although it would be wonderful to have a gun that fits your hand perfectly, that is not always the case. Learn to work with what you have. A gun that does not fit your hand exactly is not an excuse for missing!

How to acquire an Ideal Master Grip on an autoloading handgun with your strong hand

If you are right handed, your right hand is your strong hand, and your left hand is your support hand. If you are left-handed, your left hand is your strong hand, and your right hand is your support hand.

With your gun pointed in a safe direction, unload it. Perform a visual and physical inspection to confirm it is unloaded. Keep your gun pointed in a safe direction and do not allow your body parts nor those of anyone assisting you to

Chapter 3: Grip

pass in front of the muzzle.

Place your gun in your strong hand so the webbing between your thumb and index finger is positioned under the tang at the top of the back of the gun's grip (called the backstrap.)

The base of the palm of your hand and the bones of your forearm should be in a straight line directly behind the barrel of the gun.

Place your thumb in an upward position alongside the slide (on the left side of the gun if you are using your right hand, on the right side of the gun if you are using your left hand).

Your index finger, which is also your trigger finger, lies along the frame of the gun above the trigger in the register position. The rest of your fingers are wrapped around the front of the grip and tucked under the trigger guard.

This configuration, which aligns the barrel of the gun with the bones of your forearm, provides the strongest support for the gun because the bones of your wrist are locked in place and provide a straight alignment of your dominant eye

(Left) Revolver backstrap

(Right) Semiauto backstrap

and the sights. Positioning the palm of your hand and wrist directly behind the barrel also helps provide leverage for pressing the trigger. The recoil pushes directly into the base of your palm and your forearm.

This position should allow you to move your trigger (index) finger down to the trigger and place the middle of the first pad on the front side (face) of the trigger. The other segments of the trigger finger should not touch the frame of the gun when your finger is in this position, but should angle slightly outward so that there is a small space between the frame and the rest of the finger.

Remember, you are determining the fit of your handgun and should not be applying pressure to the trigger.

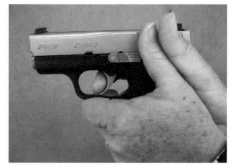

Examples of the Ideal Master Grip

What if your finger doesn't reach the trigger?

The Ideal Master Grip is simply that, an ideal configuration. It may not work for you, depending on the size of the grip of your handgun, the size of your hand and the length of your fingers. If your finger does not reach the face of the trigger, you will need to use the Modified Master Grip.

How to acquire a Modified Master Grip on an autoloading handgun with your strong hand

Before beginning this step, confirm that the gun is unloaded, that you have a safe direction in which to point it, and that none of your body parts nor those of anyone assisting you passes in front of the muzzle.

If your objective when holding the gun is to reach the trigger and fire the gun then you will need to modify your Master Grip if your trigger finger doesn't reach the trigger using the Ideal Master Grip.

Chapter 3: Grip

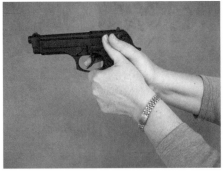 

(Left) Finger on trigger in proper position using Ideal Master Grip.
(Right) Finger that is too short to reach the trigger using Ideal Master Grip.

To do this, place your strong hand on the gun in the Ideal Master Grip, placing the tip of your trigger (index) finger as close to the front side of the trigger as possible.

Then, supporting the weight of the gun with your other hand or having someone help support it for you, rotate your strong hand around to the right or left (depending on which hand you are using), until the middle of the first pad of your trigger finger rests on the trigger face.

When you reach this point, you will see your hand is offset from the Ideal Master Grip, but this new position will become "your" Master Grip - Modified.

With your trigger finger resting in place on the trigger, wrap the rest of your fingers around the front of the grip. Your strong thumb should be in an upright position resting lightly against the slide on the left side. If your thumb is very short, it will look like it is sticking out to the side. That is fine.

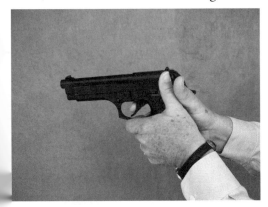 

For small hands and a large gun, the strong hand must be rotated around the grip to reach the trigger, placing the recoil on the strong thumb.

You can still have a locked wrist with a modified grip.

Shown on a revolver.

Support hand position for an autoloading handgun

Once you achieve your Ideal Master Grip or Modified Master Grip, slide your support hand onto the appropriate side of the gun by putting your support hand thumb in front of the strong hand thumb (as though the thumbs were two spoons).

Your thumbs will be together on the opposite side of the gun from your trigger finger. They will both be as upright as possible and resting against the slide. This position will not hurt your thumbs or interfere with the operation of the pistol.

Take care not to allow your thumbs to fall forward where they might interfere with your trigger finger or slide lock. If your thumb is under the slide lock when the gun fires, the knuckle can push up and lock the slide to the rear.

The thick section of your support hand palm (below your thumb) will make contact with the grip of the gun, filling in as much space along the grip as possible.

Slide your support hand upward as far as possible, so there is no gap between your thumbs and your support hand. You want your support hand to make as much contact with the grip of the gun as it can.

The support hand is just that. It provides support on the side opposite to your

Chapter 3: Grip

 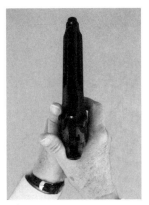

A person with small thumbs gripping a large gun.

strong hand on the gun. The support hand does this most effectively the more contact it has with the gun. Keeping your thumbs up helps stabilize the slide and barrel to keep the sights aligned. Full contact between the meaty part of your palm and the grip of the gun, with the rest of your fingers wrapped around the front of the grip, provides stability for sight alignment, leverage for pressing the trigger and control during and after recoil.

> **Tip**
>
> If your thumbs are very short, your support thumb will be more upright and your strong thumb will appear to make an X with the support thumb.

Small hands

If you use the Modified Master Grip because your hands are small, you must be especially careful to press the trigger smoothly. With your hand rotated around the side of the grip, you may have little support directly behind the gun. This may compromise your leverage capability when pressing the trigger. There is nothing you can do about it except look at it as a speed bump to get past. You must learn to press the trigger smoothly using whatever leverage is available from the portion of your thumb or hand that is on the back strap. The position of your support hand, as high as possible, is very important.

Some things to keep in mind about your grip on the gun

Keep your grip on the gun firm but not so tight that your finger tips and knuckles turn white.

You will find your grip on the gun will feel more comfortable and secure the higher you position your strong hand under the tang and the higher you position your support hand on the grip. You will be able to control your trigger press and sight alignment, bring the front sight back on target, realign the sights, catch the link and hold onto the gun during recoil.

Never allow your left or support thumb to slip behind the hammer or slide as it will be cut when the gun fires and the hammer or slide moves backwards. Remember to keep both thumbs pointed up. They may make light contact with the slide, but this will not hurt your thumbs or interfere with the operation of the pistol.

Take care not to allow your thumbs to fall forward where they might interfere with your trigger finger or slide lock. If the thumb is under the slide lock when the gun fires, the knuckle can push the lever up and lock the slide to the rear.

How closely you can follow the directions above will depend on the size and shape of your hand and fingers. Your grip may not look exactly like the pictures, but you can still shoot well.

Gap in the support fingers.

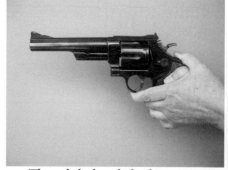

Thumb behind the hammer.

Grip too low.

Thumbs down.

Chapter 3: Grip

Thumb behind the hammer, in the way of the slide.

Locked wrist versus limp wrist

When you lock your wrist, you provide support for the recoil of your autoloading handgun. The slide moves backward after the gun fires to eject the empty case and then moves forward to strip a new round of ammunition off the top of the magazine. The energy for this is provided when the gun fires.

If your wrist is not locked, there may not be enough support for the energy to push against. If there is not enough support, a spring in the slide fails to compress, which weakens the movement of the slide. This may result in a failure of the empty case to eject from the chamber, an empty case being caught in the ejection port or a failure to feed a new round into the chamber. All of these conditions constitute a stoppage for your gun. Not a good thing!

Locking your wrist is not about gripping your gun harder. It is about increasing the tension between your hand and arm so they move as one unit.

The same problem may occur even if your wrist is locked, but you have to rotate your strong hand around so far on the side of the grip that there is little support left directly behind the barrel on the back strap. The heel of your palm and your wrist may be at an angle to the grip instead of directly behind it. There

Locked wrist

Limp wrist

25

is nothing you can do about the size of your hand. It is a speed bump to get past. Keep your wrist locked the best you can and perhaps lock your elbow on your strong arm as well.

What helped

A law enforcement officer with 15 years of shooting experience was often laughed at because of her poor performance. Her gun did not fit her hands when she used the grip she had been taught. She could not put the entire pad of her finger on the trigger face. Every time she pressed the trigger, she pushed the front sight out of alignment.

No one told her to modify her grip by turning her hand, so she struggled to shoot using a grip that only put her finger on the edge of the trigger. Her instructor never thought to tell her to modify her grip. It never occurred to him. It did not occur to her because she did not realize she could grip her gun differently from the way she had been taught.

She read our book, *Teaching Women To Shoot: A Law Enforcement Instructor's Guide* and discovered she could rotate her hand until her finger reached the trigger face. Using the Modified Master grip, she could control the trigger and sights and hit accurately.

She has gone on to share her knowledge with other female officers as well as her instructor. She actually enjoys shooting now!

Good revolver grip.

Grip for a revolver

On a revolver, your strong hand should be as high as possible on the backstrap without being in the way of the hammer. Fold your strong thumb down on the support side of the revolver.

Chapter 3: Grip

Your strong hand fingers wrap around the front of the grip. Your support hand fingers wrap around your strong hand fingers on the front of the grip, with the support hand index finger tucked under the trigger guard. Both thumbs can be folded or crossed and may point down as long as they do not interfere with your trigger finger.

Good high grip.

Grip is too low.

Hand placement and muzzle movement

Your grip affects the upward movement or muzzle flip. A good grip places your strong hand as high as possible on the backstrap of the gun to minimize the vertical distance between your hand and the barrel. The smaller this distance is, the less the gun will pivot upward in your hand.

A low grip increases the amount of force placed on your wrist when the gun fires and increases the distance the muzzle moves. You may find yourself readjusting your grip after every shot. This makes it difficult to shoot rapidly with accuracy. Apply firm pressure to your grip so you can hang on during recoil.

Lock your wrist to maintain a consistent grip and let your hand and arm move as a unit. Having your wrist locked allows the recoil energy to be absorbed along your arm and transferred to your body.

Using the magazine release button or decocking lever

Whatever position you end up using for your hands, you need to slightly rotate your right hand around the grip to the left in order to reach the magazine release button or the decocking lever with your right thumb. Always learn to use your right thumb to do these things.

If you are left-handed, you use your index or trigger finger to push the magazine release or decocking lever on most handguns.

(Upper left) Ideal Master Grip.

(Upper right) Rotated hand to reach decocking lever.

(Left) Rotated hand to reach slide lock.

Chapter 4

Sight Alignment

Sight alignment is the process of using your good stance and grip to bring your gun to eye level while you position your eye, the rear sight, front sight and the target in a straight line. Keeping this sight alignment in place and aiming at the spot you want to hit while you press the trigger determines whether the shot will be a hit or miss.

The front and rear sights allow you to aim your handgun, lining up the bore of the barrel of your handgun with the target. When the sights are properly aligned, the barrel points straight at the spot on the target you want to hit. When the gun fires, the bullet will travel down the barrel, exit and speeds toward the target to hit the spot on the target at which the sights were aimed.

There is a straight line from her eye, the rear sight, front sight and the target.

There is a spatial relationship between your eyes, the handgun, the sights, the target and where the bullet hits the target. The bullet does not get to the spot on the target you want to hit because you point your gun in that direction, press the trigger and hope. It takes a deliberate alignment of the sights with your eye and the target, which must be maintained while you press the trigger and make the shot. If you do this, the shot will be a hit. If you do not maintain the proper spatial relationship, you will miss.

Location of the sights

The sights are located on top of the slide on an autoloader or directly on top of

the barrel of a revolver. They come in a variety of sizes, shapes and even colors. Examine the sights on your gun, find where they are located and determine what they look like.

On the range, with your gun pointed in a safe direction down range, setup using your good grip and stance. With your trigger finger in the register position, bring your handgun to eye level. The first object you will see on the top of the gun is the rear sight. Further along the top of the gun (near the front end of the barrel or slide) you will see the front sight. As you look past the front sight, you should see the target downrange.

How to acquire proper sight alignment

1. Look at your target downrange. This automatically establishs a straight line between your eye and the target.
2. Using your good grip and with your trigger finger in the register position, bring the gun to eye level.
3. The rear and front sights will become points along the line between your eye and the target.
4. Confirm the proper alignment of the front sight with the rear sight. The top of the front sight is even with the top of the rear sight and the front sight is centered in the rear sight. In other words, when you look at the front sight

Chapter 4: Sight Alignment

through the rear sight, you should be able to draw a straight line across the top of the two sights. There should be equal amounts of space on each side of the front sight as it is framed by the rear sight.

5. While maintaining this alignment, be sure the front sight is aimed at the spot on the target that you want to hit.
6. See the Launch Platform chapter for a description of how to take a shot while maintaining and confirming your sight alignment.

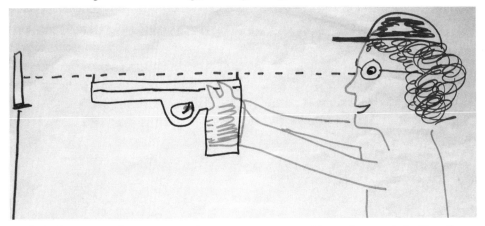

Vicki's drawing of a person sighting on a target. Note the straight line from eye to target, with the rear and front sights intersecting this straight line.

Notice in the picture below how there is an equal amount of light on either side of the front sight. Our eyes are good at centering objects, so you should find the front sight settles in the middle without much conscious thought.

How your eye focuses on the sights and target

It is important to understand that our eyes can only focus at one distance at a time. This is why not everything will be clear or in focus when you are holding your gun at eye level and looking toward the target through the sights.

31

For example, if you hold the gun at eye level and look through the sights at a paper target several yards away with an X drawn on it, the X will be sharply in focus but the rear and front sights will be slightly blurred. If you concentrate on looking at the front sight, it will be crisp and clear while the X drawn on the target appears fuzzy. If you want the shot you take to be a hit, the front sight must be as focused as your eye allows.

You will be eager to see where you hit the target, but train yourself to focus on the front sight while you press the trigger. If you change your focus to look at the target or lift your head to look over the sights to see the target as you fire, the position of the front sight will change and you will miss. Your goal is to be able to make consistently accurate hits so you will deveop the confidence that wherever you have decided your point of aim (point of aim is another way to say the spot the front sight is pointed at) is, that is where you *will* hit.

The rear sight is fuzzy because your eye should focus on the front sight.

Younger people with good eyesight may think they see all three items in focus at once but what is really happening is their eyes are shifting focus very quickly from one distance to another.

Technique Tip

Focus on the front sight, because it is the most critical element of sight alignment. Keep your eye focused on the front sight during the entire time you press the trigger, to continually confirm its alignment with the rear sight. If you are looking at the target (hoping to see where you hit) as you press the trigger, your front sight will move and you will miss.

Chapter 4: Sight Alignment

Holding steady: what helped

After hearing this description of sight alignment in a class with us, a female deputy sheriff told us she never understood the front sight needed to be aligned with the rear sight. Her instructors always assumed she knew what sight alignment was, so they always told her to watch the front sight. When Vicki drew a stick picture showing the relationship between your eye, the target and the rear and front sight, she was surprised that she had never had this explained in a manner she understood. She was a little upset that all of the missing she had been doing over the years was unnecessary and delighted that it could be corrected!

While it is important to hold your gun as steady as you can, no one can hold a pistol completely still. There will always be a certain amount of movement of your handgun. If this movement is kept within the desired target area, and you maintain the sight alignment, you will still be able to hit with some precision. This means that even when your hands are shaky, you can still make accurate hits.

Sight alignment and trigger press

When you make the decision to take a shot, confirming the sights are aligned and pressing the trigger are done simultaneously.

Remember, wherever the front sight is pointed at the target when the bullet leaves the barrel is where it will hit the target. If you do not confirm the relationship between the front and rear sight while you press the trigger, you will probably not hit your desired spot on the target. In other words you will miss.

We have found many women who consider sight alignment and trigger press as two separate operations. For example, they carefully align the sights then shift their focus to look at the target as they press the trigger. This will most likely result in a miss because the front sight will move and will no longer be aligned with the rear sight. You need to train yourself to maintain your focus on the front sight *while* you carefully apply pressure to the trigger. This takes a bit of concentration. In time you will start to feel what your body does when you press the trigger. Remind yourself that the position of the front sight on the target when the gun fires determines where the bullet strikes the target.

Women Learning To Shoot: A Guide for Law Enforcement Officers

What helped

During a chance meeting at a conference, a young girl told Vicki she was learning to be a competitive shooter. During a brief conversation, she told Vicki she thought aligning the sights and pressing the trigger were two separate actions. This is how she interpreted what her instructor had told her. She listened and did exactly as he instructed. First she aligned the sights and then she proceeded to think about the trigger press giving no more thought to the sights. She wanted to know why she missed so often. She thought maybe Vicki could explain it to her because Vicki was a woman and could help her understand.

What happens when sights are not aligned?

The picture below shows the barrel pointed up. This is what you see when the front sight is higher than the rear sight. When the front sight is higher than the rear sight, the bullet will hit high on the target.

 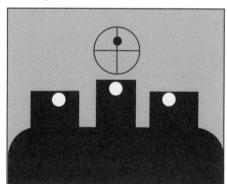

The picture below shows the barrel pointed down. This is what you see when the front sight is lower than the rear sight. When the front sight is lower than the rear sight, the bullet will hit low on the target.

 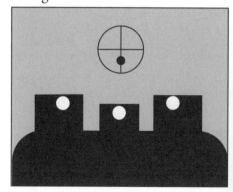

Chapter 4: Sight Alignment

When the front sight is shifted to the right, the bullet will hit to the right of the target.

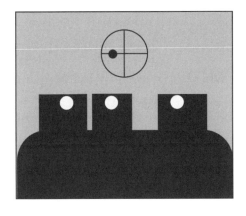

When the front sight is shifted to the left, the bullet will hit to the left of the target.

What happened

Many officers have tried to improve their hit percentage by compensating where they put their front sight, high and right to make up for poorly aligned sights, jerking the trigger or flinching. The worse cases we have encountered are when the firearms instructor suggests to the officers that they compensate for their misses by moving their point of aim on the target, usually high and to the right. The instructor is sure when they miss and push the shot low and left that it will hit somewhere near the center of the target. *Trying to correct an error by committing another error never works!* This may allow the officer to pass her firearms qualification test but what is going to happen when she faces a real bad guy who is shooting at her?

> "We start our qualification course at 25 yards and as I walk forward I see how bad my shots are. I know I will not pass and just want to get this over with and leave as soon as possible."

Women Learning To Shoot: A Guide for Law Enforcement Officers

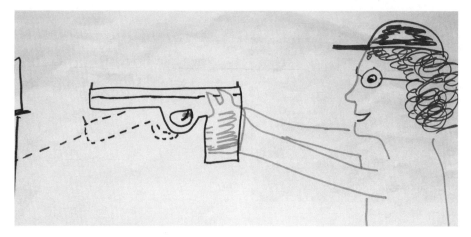

Vicki's drawing of what happens when you contract your entire hand or jerk the trigger. The front sight moves down and to the left.

Do you do this?

During a firearms class for female officers, we ask them to place an X on the target to show where they put their front sight to make center-of-mass hits. None of the officers placed their X in the center mass area of the target. Some were just over the shoulder, some were by the ear and some were three or four inches high and to the right of the center of the target. One officer told us she placed her front sight differently depending on the distance they were shooting. These female officers had between 2 and 10 years of service. None were able to specifically tell us why they did not aim where they wanted to hit. They only knew that if they aimed at the center of the target, that is *not* where they hit. Sometimes, although not always, if they aimed somewhere else, they *might* hit the center of the target! Clearly they had never had the spatial relationship of their eye, the gun, the sights and the target explained to them so they could understand it.

Chapter 4: Sight Alignment

Trajectory

The distance between the rear and front sight is usually only a few inches. This distance is dictated by the size of the gun. The distance from the front sight to the target is measured in feet or yards and is always variable.

If the front sight moves even a fraction of an inch between the time you create the sight alignment and the moment you press the trigger, the bullet will miss by inches by the time it reaches the target.

"I can shoot straight if I don't have to shoot too far," Scarlett O'Hara said as she headed out alone into the woods in her buggy in the movie *Gone With the Wind*.

You may shoot well at three or even seven yards but fall apart at the 15-yard line. The farther away from the target you are, the more critical it is for you to align your sights properly and then *continually confirm your sight alignment while you press the trigger!*

Consistently missing the target?

Sometimes the problem is the sights, but not often. Front sights can come loose or fall off. Adjustable rear sights and even fixed sights can be knocked out of alignment. Be sure you are sighting correctly before trying to adjust the sights on your gun. Be sure the sights are secure and positioned properly. If you are unfamiliar, ask someone who should know, such as an armorer.

Do not use the sights as an excuse for missing. If immediately necessary, it is possible to hit accurately without either a front or rear sight. Sights can fly off guns while you are shooting!

Types of sights

The rear sight usually appears as three sides of a square with the top missing. Or the corners may be rounded so it looks like a "u" shape. The color is almost always black but there may be dots on each side or a white line outlining the shape. The dots may be white or appear colorless in daylight but glow (green or other colors) in low light if they are night sights.

Glock rear sight with white outline.

The front sight usually appears as a rectangle sticking up from the slide and is often called a post. Front sights most often are black, but may also have a dot, which may be white or any other color. The dot may appear colorless in daylight but glow in low light if it is a night sight.

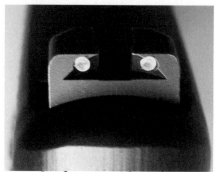

Sig factory night sights.

Some front sights are not a post but a ramp. Seen from the side, the sight looks like a triangle but viewed through the rear sight, it actually looks like the post.

The rear sight can be as simple as a notch cut into the top of the barrel or slide. The rear sight can also be a solid piece of metal in the shape of a "u" or a square with the top missing. It is attached to the top of the gun, either with a pin that goes through the sight and down into the top of the barrel, or the sight slides into a groove on top of the slide and is secured with glue. This type of rear sight is not adjustable and is called a fixed sight. As long as fixed sights are tightly in place, they should be accurate. If the fixed sights are loose or come off, have them repaired by an armorer or gunsmith.

Front sight with an insert on a S&W revolver.

Other types of rear sights are adjustable. There is a mechanism, which may look like a screw, that allows you to move the rear sight to the right or left and up or down to change the point of impact on the target.

The purpose of the rear sight is to provide an opening through which to view the

Adjustable rear sight. Screw adjusts left to right.

Chapter 4: Sight Alignment

front sight. The rear sight is used as a reference point when you align the front sight. Since your eye does not focus directly on the rear sights, they come with a variety of visual aids. Some sights are flat black, some have an outline of white, while others have a dot on each side or below.

The front sight is usually a small vertical rectangle positioned on top of the barrel or slide near the muzzle. It can be the same color as the gun, painted a bright color or have a dot just below the top. Some people prefer a solid black rear and front sight while others find the three dot system easier to use. Some people find the dots and lines or color helpful, others do not. We suggest you look at several types to determine which is easiest for you to see. Regardless of the style, the sights are all used the same way.

> If your technique is poor, you will not shoot well, no matter how precise the sights are.

What happened

Two officers from a federal agency came to the range. The woman had been referred for remedial training and the man just wanted some extra practice. Both officers started out at seven yards then moved to fifteen yards, shooting at paper targets. The officer who was there for practice had a consistent group at both distances so he switched to the steel plate rack. The other officer had a more scattered group at fifteen yards and continued working on paper targets. What happened next really surprised us. We were not watching the officer shooting the plate rack, but we could hear what was going on. He fired several shots before he finally hit a steel plate. This pattern continued for all six targets. How could he miss the steel plate when he had such a good group on the paper target?

He was honest enough to tell us when he shot the paper targets, he placed his front sight slightly high and to the right of the center of the target. Basically he had solved his shooting problem by moving where he pointed the sights. He was so used to shooting at paper that he could easily figure out just where to put the sights to make center of the target hits. When he moved to the steel plates he did not have a reference point to place his sight and of course he missed the target. This officer had no trouble passing his firearms qualification course and the firearms instructors at his agency probably had no idea that he had failed to master the skill of sight alignment and trigger press.

Chapter 5

Trigger Control

Trigger control and sight alignment are the two most important elements of accurate shooting. You can have perfect sight alignment and still miss your target if you move the gun too much when you press the trigger and the front sight does not stay on the spot you want the bullet to hit. Or you may press the trigger with perfect smoothness but still miss because you failed to use your sights while you pressed the trigger.

> There is a spatial relationship between you, the gun, the bullet and the target. That means any movement of one of the four affects the other three. Done correctly, you hit the target. Done incorrectly, you miss.

A controlled trigger press is a learned skill. You need to be aware of what your body is doing and learn to control your muscles. Your job is to minimize the movement of the gun by holding it steady and allowing only your trigger finger to move when pressing the trigger. The rest of your strong hand and your entire support hand provide support for the gun. Over time, your finger will develop muscle memory and press smoothly while you maintain proper sight alignment.

This is easier said than done. After all, our brain knows that when we press the trigger, the gun will fire, creating a loud noise and upward motion of the gun, or recoil. It is natural for us to react to this noise and recoil – every shooter does. We may react before, during or after the shot is fired. These reactions are commonly referred to as anticipation, jerking the trigger or flinching. Your eyes may even close involuntarily!

> **Tip**
> Your finger goes on the trigger only when you have aligned the sights on the target and have decided to shoot!

Women Learning To Shoot: A Guide for Law Enforcement Officers

To be a competent shooter, you need to learn what happens mechanically when you press the trigger and control your reaction to it. Your job is to control your body as it stabilizes the gun. You then press the trigger and the bullet leaves the gun. You know in advance there will be recoil and noise. You have to ignore both. Your mental focus must be on the process of holding the gun steady, pressing the trigger and keeping the sights aligned. If you do that, you will make a hit. If you think with dread about the recoil and noise, you will miss.

> This is the hard part. It is easy to push the front sight out of alignment when applying pressure to the trigger. Moving the front sight out of alignment is the number one reason for failing to accurately hit the target. Remember, wherever the front sight is pointed is where the bullet will go. If the front sight is not on the target, the bullet will not hit the target, it will miss.

Trigger finger placement

The exact position where you need to place your finger on the face of the trigger depends on the amount of pressure (measured in pounds) it takes to move the trigger and the distance the trigger must move (or travel) to complete the internal mechanical processes and fire the gun. Correct placement of your finger on the trigger allows you to press straight back, rather than pushing or pulling the trigger to one side or the other.

(Left) Where Vicki must place her right hand in order for her trigger finger to reach the trigger. (Right) The ideal placement for Vicki's right hand. She cannot reach the trigger from this position.

Chapter 5: Trigger Control

Where you "need" to place your finger and where you "can" place your finger may be two different things depending on the fit of the gun. You may have to adjust your grip so your finger will be in the best spot on the trigger for a smooth trigger press.

Trigger weights

The information below describes how a trigger feels when it is pressed. To simplify this subject, we define trigger press as light, medium or heavy in weight. The distance the trigger travels when pressed is defined as short, intermediate or long.

Many handgun triggers feel the same for every shot. Some, such as a double-action autoloading handgun, will have a long, heavy trigger press for the first shot and then a light, short press for subsequent shots.

The amount of pressure needed to press the trigger all the way back and fire the gun is measured in pounds.

- Light - less than five pounds (less than five pounds is very light and not recommended for defensive handguns)
- Medium - six to nine pounds
- Heavy - ten pounds or more

How far a trigger travels:

- Short - less than half an inch
- Intermediate - one half inch
- Long - three-quarters of an inch or more

> **Tip**
>
> There are only two places for your trigger finger. It should either be in the register position resting alongside the frame above the trigger guard when you are not shooting, or in contact with the trigger if you have made the decision to shoot. Never allow your trigger finger to float in thin air near the trigger.

A Smith & Wesson 1911 with a light trigger.

A Glock with a medium trigger.

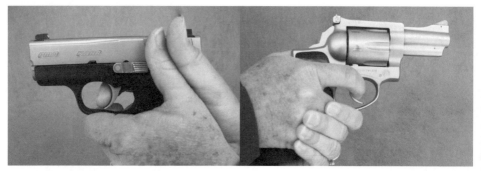
A Kahr PM9 with a heavy trigger.   A revolver with a heavy trigger.

A light or medium trigger

If your trigger only takes a few pounds of pressure to move, center the pad of your finger on the trigger about half way between the tip of your finger and the first joint.

A heavy trigger

If the trigger on your handgun is heavier, you will need more leverage to press it back. Push the tip of your trigger finger across the trigger until the right edge (if you are left handed, the left edge) of the trigger presses into the first joint.

Exception

Vicki has very small hands. She will use the tip of her finger when she is shooting a large gun with a heavy trigger. If she rotates her hand far enough to place the first joint of her trigger finger against the face of the trigger, she does not have enough leverage to press the trigger.

Chapter 5: Trigger Control

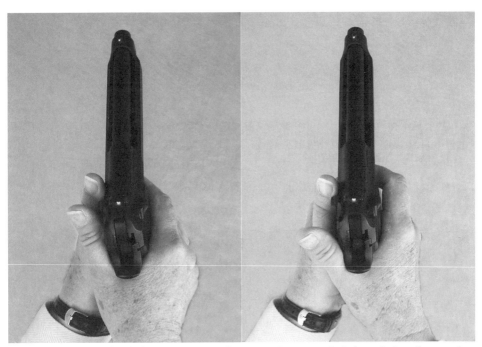

The Beretta on the left is positioned correctly in Vicki's hand, but her index finger cannot reach the trigger. To shoot this gun, she must rotate her right hand around the grip and rest the backstrap on the base of her thumb.

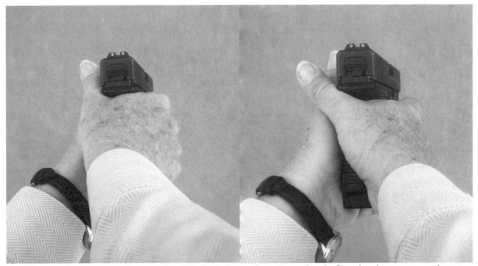

A Glock that is too large for Vicki's hands. On the left, she has a good grip, but cannot reach the trigger. Rotating her hand around the grip to get a good trigger pull concentrates the recoil on the base of her thumb.

Problems

When the gun is too large for your hand, you will have to rotate your hand around the grip in order to obtain a proper trigger finger placement. If you can barely reach the trigger using a proper grip, you will probably end up pressing the trigger with the tip of your finger. This will cause you to push the trigger to the side and push the muzzle and front sight out of alignment, causing a miss. In other words, the front sight moves laterally to the side and causes the bullet to miss the target.

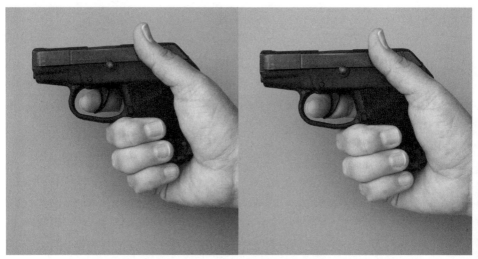

Shooting a gun that is too small encourages you to put too much finger through the trigger guard, as at right.

When a gun is too small for your hand, you may slip too much finger across the trigger. If you have too much of your finger across the trigger, the tendency is to pull the muzzle of the gun to one side as you press the trigger. This can pull the muzzle laterally, moving the front sight out of alignment, and cause you to miss your target.

(Left) Sight pulled to the right.

(Right) Sight pushed to the left.

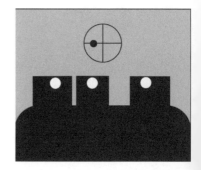

Chapter 5: Trigger Control

Trigger press

We use the term "press" because it provides the mental image of the index finger doing an isolated task, such as pressing the shutter button on a camera. We find the term squeeze creates a mental picture of using your entire hand to squeeze something, such as a lemon. When you think "squeeze," your entire hand will react. If your whole hand squeezes, you will pull the front sight down. Press the trigger with just your trigger finger while the rest of your hand maintains steady supporting pressure on the grip.

The idea is to maintain constant pressure on the grip with your hand and only use your trigger finger to press the trigger. Press the trigger straight back using smooth continuous pressure with only your trigger finger moving.

When you place your trigger finger on the trigger and begin to press, it first moves with little resistance. This is called "the slack." You are "taking up the slack" when you press the trigger without resistance. You must do this with a smooth steady motion until there is significant resistance.

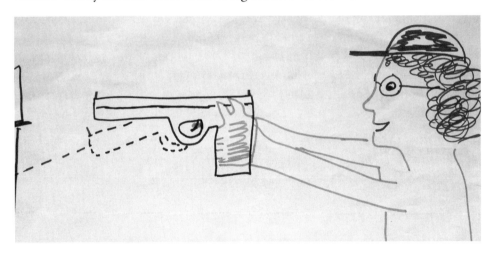

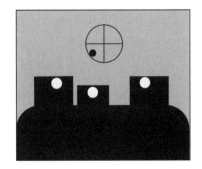

(Above) Drawing showing the front sight moving when the hand contracts. (Right) How the sights might look if you contract your hand.

Press smoothly through the resistance just as you do when you take up the slack. If you rush by jerking or slapping or snapping the trigger, the bullet will miss, because the front sight will move. It takes focused concentration to train your trigger finger to apply continual smooth pressure until the gun fires. It is very important to press smoothly and simultaneously watch the sights.

You may find yourself contracting your entire hand if you do not have a great deal of strength. If you can only get the tip of your finger on the trigger, you will probably try to "help" press the trigger by contracting one or both of your hands. Don't do this! Concentrate on pressing as smoothly as possible.

Be very careful that you do not start to squeeze with your whole hand as you try to go fast and reduce your shot-to-shot time!

Putting it together

It is not uncommon for the entire body to move in anticipation of firing the gun. What you have to do is will your body to remain still and only move your trigger finger. This means ignoring the actual noise and recoil. Press the trigger using a smooth continuous pressure as the trigger moves to the rear and completes the mechanical process that fires the gun. Pay attention to what the muscles in your hands are doing. Keep your eye focused on the front sight to continually confirm proper alignment. The target will not be in clear focus. Remember that the trigger press and sight alignment are done simultaneously.

It takes time to learn the muscle control necessary to make each shot smooth and accurate. When you fire multiple shots, a technique that dramatically improves accuracy and speed is called catching the link, continuous trigger contact or trigger reset.

Continuous trigger contact or trigger reset

Continuous trigger contact is a technique that will dramatically improve your accuracy and speed when firing multiple shots. Here is how it works.

1. When you press the trigger to fire the gun, hold the trigger all the way to the rear as the gun fires and recoils.
2. Keep the trigger pressed to the rear as you realign the sights for your next shot.
3. Once the sights are realigned, allow the trigger to move forward until you feel and hear a click. This is the trigger sear being reset, enabling the gun

Chapter 5: Trigger Control

to fire again. This click is defined as the link or trigger reset, or catching the link.

Your finger never loses contact with the trigger as the gun fires. This helps to minimize the distance the finger travels and it minimizes the movement of the gun. Continuous trigger contact also improves speed between shots and the accuracy of those shots. In other words it improves your trigger control.

(Left) beginning the trigger stroke. (Right) the gun has fired and the shooter holds the trigger back until the sights are realigned.

With sights reacquired, release the trigger until it resets, then begin the next trigger stroke.

Resist the temptation to let your trigger finger come too far forward, allowing it to lose contact with the trigger. The next trigger pull will crash into the trigger, causing the sights to move and the shot to miss.

How does it do this? It gives you the shortest possible distance for the trigger to travel between shots. It helps you keep your trigger press smooth because your finger is in constant contact and not in danger of bashing into the trigger as it would if you take your finger off the trigger and then try to find it again quickly. Bashing the trigger may push the front sight out of alignment.

The following drill helps you practice continuous trigger contact or trigger reset. You need to work with a partner. Make sure you are using an unloaded handgun and keep it pointed in a safe direction.

Take a dry fire shot and hold the trigger to the rear while your partner manually pulls the slide back and lets it go. (This is necessary to reset the sear.)

Slowly release the pressure on the trigger allowing it to move forward until you hear or feel a click, then press the trigger back for the next dry fire shot. Repeat this several times.

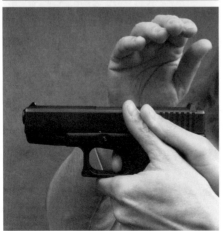

Practicing catching the link with a partner. After you dry-fire, your partner pulls the slide to the rear, recocking the gun. You continue to hold the trigger to the rear while the slide cycles. Your partner releases the slide (not riding it forward) and allows it to return to battery. You allow the trigger to move forward until it resets, then take the next shot.

Chapter 5: Trigger Control

Hearing or feeling the click when the trigger resets is more pronounced on some models such as Glocks. Single action autoloaders such as a Colt or Browning system have a less distinctive click or a short reset that is hard to feel.

On revolvers, the trigger must travel all the way forward after each shot due to the design of the internal firing mechanism, but the trigger finger still maintains contact. This is also true for some self-decocking autoloaders such as the Kahr. The shot-to-shot time for these guns is inherently slower than with other autoloading pistols. The new Sig DAK trigger actually has two links or clicks and the gun can be fired from either position.

Exercises to improve trigger control

This exercise helps build a new neuropath for your trigger finger. Your trigger finger needs to learn (develop a new neuropath) to work independently of your other fingers. It needs to learn to press the trigger, not squeeze the trigger by using the rest of your fingers and hand.

Hold your strong hand out with your fingers separated. Touch your index finger to your thumb. Your goal is to move your index finger without moving your other fingers. Minimize any movement of your other fingers. Practice this exercise to build independence for your trigger finger.

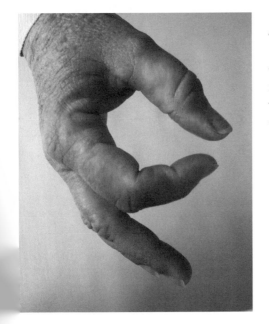

Trigger finger control exercise.

Simulate a trigger pull with your index finger, touching your thumb while minimizing any movement of the other fingers.

Strength exercise

A simple way to develop strength in your trigger finger without contracting your whole hand is to use a spray bottle. You can grip it with your hand to practice maintaining a consistent grip while only moving your trigger finger.

An empty spray bottle works well or you can fill the bottle with some water to simulate the weight of your handgun. Using your usual good stance and grip, bring the bottle to eye level. Press the trigger so only your trigger finger moves. If you notice the bottle moving or the water sloshing, you are moving more than your trigger finger.

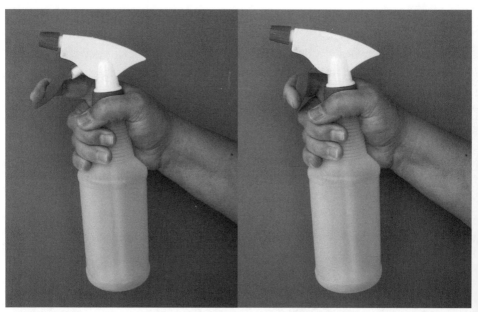

Operate the trigger of the squirt bottle without moving any other fingers or the bottle at all. Learn to operate the trigger finger independently. Add water for added resistence.

Chapter 5: Trigger Control

> **Examples of the most common types of triggers**
>
> The 1911 is an example of a handgun with a short, light trigger press that is the same for every shot.
>
> The Glock is an example of a handgun with an intermediate, medium press that is the same for every shot.
>
> A double action revolver is an example of a handgun with a long, heavy trigger press that is the same for every shot (in double action mode.)
>
> A Sig Sauer 239 with a standard double action trigger or Beretta 92 is an example of a handgun that has a long, heavy trigger press for the first shot and a short, light trigger press for subsequent shots.
>
> A double-action-only autoloader is an example of a handgun with a long, heavy trigger press that is the same for every shot.

Chapter 6

Launch Platform

You are the Launch Platform for the gun. The gun does the work of pushing the bullet out of the barrel, but your job is to hold the gun steady and align the sights and continue to align them on the spot you want to hit as you press the trigger in order to have an accurate hit. Holding the sights in alignment and pressing the trigger must be done simultaneously once you have made the decision to fire. The bullet will land where the front sight is pointed at the moment the gun goes bang. Sight alignment and trigger press are simultaneous events, not separate events done sequentially.

Do not align the sights and then forget about them while you press the trigger!

This is the basic routine you need to learn to develop consistently accurate shooting skills. You must also understand that there is a spatial relationship between you, your gun and the target. In other words, what your eyes are doing, what your hands are doing and what your trigger finger is doing all affect the gun, the sights and where the bullet will hit. Once you understand this process, any time you start to miss, you can review in your mind all of the fundamentals of the "Launch Platform" and correct the problem yourself.

Remember to keep your finger in the register position (laying alongside the frame above the trigger.) The trigger finger only comes in contact with the trigger when the decision to fire the gun has been made.

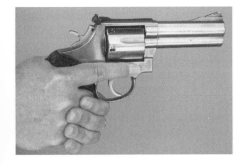

Women Learning To Shoot: A Guide for Law Enforcement Officers

Now how do you do this?

When you are on line, facing down range:

1. Look at the target and create a straight line between your eye and the target.

2. Facing down range, looking at the target with the handgun in your hand using your usual good grip and stance, bring the gun upward until the rear and front sights intersect the line between your eye and the target.

3. Once the front and rear sight intersect the line between your eye and the target, shift your visual focus to the front sight and align it with the rear sight. The front sight is framed by the rear sight and the front and rear sights are level across the top. The front sight will be in focus. The rear sight and the target are visible but not as sharply focused as the front sight.

4. This relationship of your eye, the sights and target in a straight line is the alignment that must be maintained while pressing the trigger to assure an accurate hit. Maintain awareness of the target but understand it will not be in focus.

5. Your focus will be on the front sight. Continually monitor the relationship between the front and rear sight, keeping the tops of the rear and front sight level. Always maintain awareness of the target even if it is not in sharp focus.

6. Maintain the position of the front sight on the spot you want to hit as best you can. Please understand, however, it is impossible to keep the front sight completely still. In fact, the entire gun will be moving slightly. Your goal is to keep the sights aligned and minimize movement of the gun.

7. Once you have made the decision to fire, your finger comes out of the register position and into its proper position on the trigger. Continue to align the sights as the act of placing your finger on the trigger may push the front sight out of alignment.

8. Begin pressing the trigger to the rear. Apply the pressure as smoothly as you can. Only your trigger finger moves. Avoid squeezing the trigger as your entire hand will then be applying pressure and will pull the front sight down. Continue to confirm the sight alignment the entire time you are pressing the trigger. The gun will fire when you have pressed the trigger completely to the rear and all the internal mechanical processes have been completed.

9. Once the gun has fired, recoil will push the gun upwards. Your job now is

Chapter 6: Launch Platform

to bring the sights back to the visual line between your eye and the target, realign the sights, and put the front sight back on the target. Repeat the shooting process as needed, connecting each repetition with another process known variously as continuous trigger contact, catching the link or trigger reset. This process is described in detail below. Sight alignment and trigger press are simultaneous events, not separate ones done sequentially.

10. The bullet hits exactly where you intended!

Keep your mind focused on the task of hitting the target. Keep the clutter out of your mind such as "Oh what if I miss! Oh the recoil is awful! Oh the noise is so loud!" Don't program yourself to fail! Remember, wherever the front sight is pointed on the target when the bullet leaves the barrel is where the bullet will land.

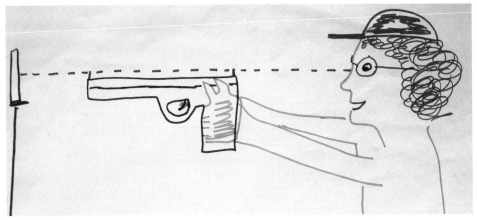

This drawing shows a straight line from the eye to the target with the front and rear sights intersecting the line.

What happens if you miss?

You think you have done all the steps listed above but at the very important moment in time when the gun goes bang, the front sight is no longer aimed at the spot you wanted to hit on the target and it hits somewhere else. This is a miss!

How does missing happen?

Any one of the following actions on your part will move the front sight out of alignment making the bullet miss the spot you wanted to hit.

1. You did not continue to confirm the sight alignment while you pressed the trigger.

2. You pressed the trigger too quickly, causing the front sight to move out of alignment at the moment the gun fired.

3. You used your whole hand to squeeze the trigger causing the front sight to move out of alignment or off the target, usually low and to the left.

4. You pressed or pulled on the side of the trigger and that motion moved the front sight off the target.

5. You lifted your head and looked over your sights at the target just before the gun fired and therefore did not utilize the sights at all. You wanted to see where the bullet hit.

6. You changed your focus from the front sight to the target and the front sight moved out of alignment.

7. You were in a hurry to fire and get it over with because of the noise and recoil.

8. You closed your eyes.

When you miss, you have to forget about that miss and focus on the next shot to make it an accurate hit. Thinking about the miss is clutter in your mind and the clutter becomes a speed bump that slows you down and gets in your way. Get over it and focus on the basics of being the Launch Platform.

When you have several accurate hits in a row, try to analyze what you are doing. What were you thinking about? What were you looking at? How are you applying pressure to the trigger? What do the sights look like? Do you remember seeing them during the entire process?

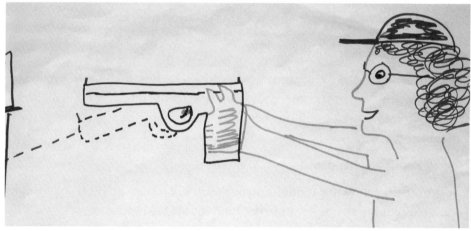

The front sight moves downward when you press the trigger too quickly.

Chapter 6: Launch Platform

What you have learned about the Launch Platform is the sequence of steps for making one accurate hit. Most of the time you need to make multiple accurate hits in a row. The sequence of steps for the Launch Platform needs to be repeated for each accurate hit. Each repetition needs to be connected with the process known variously as continuous trigger contact, catching the link or trigger reset.

> **Tracking a moving target**
>
> When shooting at a moving target, your front sight moves with the target but stays in alignment with the rear sight. Do not stop following the target when you press the trigger to take a shot. Keep the sights moving with the target.

Continuous trigger contact or trigger reset

Continuous trigger contact is a technique that will dramatically improve your accuracy and speed when firing multiple shots. Here is what you do when you are on line facing down range and firing at the target.

1. When you press the trigger and the gun fires, hold the trigger all the way to the rear as the gun recoils and the barrel rises. The slide cycles, the empty case is ejected, a new round of ammunition enters the chamber and the slide slams forward.

2. You need to continue to hold the trigger to the rear as you bring the gun down toward the target and again intersect the visual line between your eye and the target with the front and rear sights. Realign the sights for your next shot. The trigger is still held to the rear while you do this.

3. Once the sights are realigned, slowly allow the trigger to move forward until you feel and hear a click. This is the trigger sear being reset, enabling the gun to fire again. This click is defined as the link or trigger reset or catching the link. The trigger is not as far forward as it can go, but it is not necessary for it to go that far. Once you have reached the point where you hear or feel the click, the gun is ready to fire again once you make the decision to fire.

4. If you do not stop the forward movement of the trigger at the click, do not try to go back to the click! The gun will fire if you try and you may or may not have made the decision to fire at that moment! If you do not stop at the click,

simply prepare to take your next shot with the trigger all the way forward, just as it was with the first shot you took. The point is, if you have gone past the click, if you try to move the trigger back to it, the gun will fire.

Continue to confirm your sight alignment while you press the trigger for your next shot. Repeat the entire process until you can consistently stop at the click.

Your finger never loses contact with the trigger as the gun fires. This helps to minimize the distance the finger travels and it minimizes the movement of the gun. Continuous trigger contact also improves speed between shots and the accuracy of those shots. In other words it improves your trigger control.

Hold the trigger back during recoil until the sights are realigned.

When the sights are aligned, reset the trigger and start the next shot. Do not let your finger fly off the trigger.

Be sure you are programming yourself for success, not defeat. Do not press the trigger until you remind yourself of all the things you must do simultaneously to assure yourself of a hit. Do not think about it as just getting the gun to go bang. Think about it as getting the bullet to hit where you want to hit. You have to think and make it happen—not wish for it to happen.

Chapter 6: Launch Platform

> Practice catching the link in a dry fire drill with a partner. With an unloaded gun, on line facing down range, align your sights on the target. Follow the steps outlined in the Launch Platform. Your partner will cycle the slide (move it backwards and then let it go, to move forward on its own) to simulate the gun firing. You will hold the trigger to the rear while the slide is being cycled. Return the front sight to the target and realign the sights. Then, slowly allow the trigger to move forward until you hear or feel a click. Stop at that point.

Chapter 7

Recoil

Recoil is energy. It is the backward motion of your gun in response to the forward motion of the bullet moving out of the muzzle. This energy moves your body and the gun. Your gun will move straight back, pushing against your hands, arms and shoulders. The muzzle of your gun will move upward. For some this is distressing, for others it is no problem.

Anticipation of recoil, noise and pain

Everyone knows about recoil whether they have ever fired a gun or not! Everyone knows if you fire a gun there *will* be recoil. We hear hair-raising tales of noise and pain and we see it happen on TV and in movies. The first time you fire a gun you may already be convinced it is going to be awful. Sometimes it is and sometimes it is not so bad. Either way, there is an anticipation of what it will be like the next time.

Some of us do not like the noise any more than we like the push of energy. Loud, sharp or intense noises are distressing. A woman's range of hearing is greater than most men's and we often react by involuntarily jumping when we hear a loud noise. It does not matter if the noise is expected or not. If this applies to you, you may want to wear both foam ear plugs and muff-type ear protection.

When you prepare to shoot, your mind and body may try to react to the recoil motion or noise before it happens. You think if you react first perhaps it will not be so bad. If you instructor tells you that you are "anticipating, flinching or jerking the shot," it means your body is reacting to the recoil before the recoil actually hits you. You may push the muzzle forward or down as a way to "control" the recoil. In an attempt to get the shot over with as quickly as possible, you may bash into the trigger with your finger or snap it back. You may close your eyes involuntarily. Any of these will cause the front sight to be pushed out of alignment with the rear sight and the spot on the target you want to hit, and you will miss!

There may be some pain involved in recoil, but pain is a relative feeling, different for different people.

Felt recoil

Felt or perceived recoil is subjective and is different for each caliber. Two people can shoot the same gun and have completely different experiences—one may not be bothered at all while the other is uncomfortable and finds the gun unpleasant to shoot more than a few times.

Smaller calibers have less recoil than larger calibers. The 9mm and 38 Special calibers have the most controllable recoil for the most people. Many people describe the 40 S&W caliber recoil as a sharp punch or snap. The 45 ACP and 357 Sig are described as a shove or rolling motion. These perceptions depend on the frame material, model of gun and the size and shape of your hand. Large hands connected to large arms and shoulders seem to absorb the recoil more easily than small hands connected to small arms and torsos.

In general, an all-steel frame handgun is heavier and transfers less recoil to the shooter than a similar sized polymer, aluminum or titanium frame. Large frame guns are heavier and produce less recoil than compact models.

Muzzle flip

You will feel your gun move back and see the muzzle move upward when you fire your gun. These two events happen at the same time. The upward movement is called muzzle flip. How much of each of these motions is present depends on many things such as the design of your handgun, the size and weight of your gun, the material it is made of, the type of ammunition you use, how you hold your gun, your build and stature.

There is no way to avoid recoil or muzzle flip. Your job is to maintain control of your gun during recoil. Do not fight the recoil or try to anticipate it. Do not worry about it. Just keep a firm grip and let the recoil happen. If you try to stop the movement of your gun by pushing it forward or pulling it down, you will move the front sight and miss. Recoil is a speed bump. Learn to ignore it.

Managing recoil

You can manage recoil by using a good grip, keeping your wrist locked and flexing your elbows.

Chapter 7: Recoil

Examples of good grips. Strong hand is high and thumbs are pointed up.

> **Technical Tip**
> Keep your support hand high and snug against the strong-hand thumb.

Grip

A good grip places your strong hand as high as possible on the backstrap. You must minimize the vertical distance between your hand and the barrel. The smaller this distance is, the less the gun will pivot upward. This means the muzzle will return to eye level quickly with the sights ready to line up for your next shot.

This high hand position helps you maintain your grip through recoil so you do not have to readjust your hand after every shot. When your sights quickly return to eye level and your hand stays in position, you decrease the time between shots.

A low grip on your handgun increases the vertical distance between your hand and the barrel. This allows for more muzzle flip, which means it will take longer for the sights to return to eye level. If your hand is lower on the grip, more force is placed on your wrist and you may find yourself readjusting your grip after every shot. Your support hand may lose its grip or be pushed off your gun. Waiting for the muzzle to come back to eye level and readjusting your grip after each shot slows you down.

It is up to you to find the best grip configuration for your hand on your gun. Practice your grip and use the same one every time you shoot. Quickly verify your grip before you fire. Eventually your hands develop muscle memory and go to the same place every time. Learn more in Chapter 3, Grip.

Wrist

Your wrist is a very flexible joint and can rotate in several directions. You need to learn to keep your wrist from moving by contracting muscles in your hand and arms. The idea is to have your hand and arm move as a unit. This is known as a locked wrist. A locked wrist helps control the motion of the gun during recoil and it provides the necessary support for the operation of the slide on an autoloading handgun. Learn more in Chapter 3, Grip.

Elbows

Keep your elbows slightly bent so they can give or flex like a spring to absorb some of the recoil.

Size and shape of your hand

Recoil pushes the gun back into the palm and webbing of your hand. If you have small or slim hands, you will have less padding to cushion recoil. Handguns with metal, wooden or hard polymer grips can be punishing to small thin hands. Rubber grips help provide a cushion.

If you have small hands and are using a gun that does not fit properly, it will take you longer to regain control of your gun and return the front sight to the target. You may find that you have to reacquire your grip before shooting again. Try gripping firmly enough to prevent your hand from losing contact.

Hands come in all sizes. Not only are fingers different lengths, but so are palms. Hands have different thicknesses too. A slim hand, even if the fingers are long, will have greater felt recoil than a thick hand with short fingers.

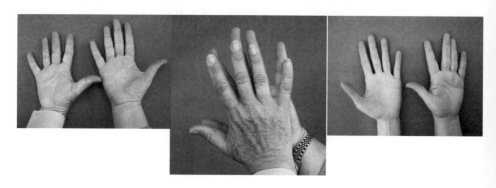

Chapter 7: Recoil

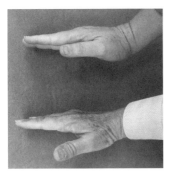 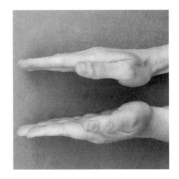

Recoil and speed

When there are no time limits, you can recover from recoil and readjust your grip between shots with no consequences. When you are required to fire multiple shots in a limited amount of time, you have to be able to recover from recoil quickly. If you try to shoot before your sights are aligned or you jerk the trigger trying to shoot fast, you will miss. Use the techniques described in the Launch Platform (Chapter 6) and learn to ignore the recoil. Keep your grip strong and secure to maintain control.

The caliber, frame size, frame material, your hand size and thickness will all determine how quickly you recover and are ready to fire the next shot. Clear the clutter from your mind the best you can. You may not be able to change your gun and you cannot change your hand size, but you can focus on your goal of hitting the target accurately!

> **Technical Tip**
>
> Changing your grip covers may change how the gun fits your hand or how well you can hang on. You may change to bigger grips, smaller grips, smoother or softer grips or textured grips. Choose those that help you maintain a proper and effective grip while shooting.

Does this happen to you?

A smaller-statured woman shooting a 40 caliber handgun with a large grip may manage the recoil and have accurate hits for a number of shots before the effects of recoil start to accumulate. The slow recovery from recoil becomes more pronounced as her shoulders, arms and hands become fatigued. The usual result is that she starts mashing the trigger to get the next shot or shots over with as quickly as possible.

What happened

The combination of the type of handgun you use and the size and shape of your hands can create painful recoil. A former Army officer and paratrooper found a Glock 36 (45ACP) fit her well, but after firing several magazines, her group started to open up (the hits were not as close together). She has long, thin hands and the sharp recoil of the Glock caused her to develop a flinch. When she tried a Colt Commander in 9mm, she was able to regularly fire over 100 rounds without flinching.

An officer with thin hands had trouble using her 40 caliber handgun. She understood the fundamentals of shooting and the gun fit her well, but after firing two or three magazines, she started flinching. The flinch was in response to the pain caused by the sharp recoil. When she switched to a 9mm, she was able to complete a day on the range firing several hundred rounds without flinching.

What helped

Shooting a handgun when the grip is too large for your hand can cause pain when you have to hold on tightly during recoil. After Vicki switched from a 9mm to a 40 caliber handgun, she developed a pain in her arm between the wrist and elbow that slowly got worse. It reached the point where she had trouble picking up a glass of water. She was diagnosed with tendonitis of the muscle called the *extensor carpi radialis brevis*, a condition commonly known as tennis elbow.

In Vicki's case, it was brought on by repetitive use. She had to increase the amount of force she used to grip the gun as she dealt with the increased recoil produced by the 40 caliber gun. The doctor advised Vicki to rest her arm by not shooting and to wear a brace to massage the area to relieve the pain. She was also given stretching and strengthening exercises to condition the muscles. Eventually her arm improved.

Emotional reactions to shooting

Movement is only one part of what you experience when you are shooting. Guns create loud noise when fired and you can be startled when you fire your gun or by the noise of other guns. You may involuntarily tense your body, jump or your heart may start pounding. All of these are natural reactions. After you fire several rounds, you will learn what your gun sounds like and your startle

Chapter 7: Recoil

reaction will diminish.

We have had a few women who experience strong emotions when startled. For example, a woman burst into tears the first time she fired her gun because the noise was so disconcerting. The fact that the noise did not "hurt" her is of little significance since the reaction is involuntary. When she wore both ear plugs and muffs, the noise was lessened and she was more comfortable.

> **Technical Tip**
>
> Women have sensitive ears. Make sure you have good hearing protection and it fits. Use foam ear plugs and muffs if necessary.

What happened

Maria had only been shooting a few times with her boyfriend. She admitted to us that she was still scared of handguns. We soon learned that the loud abrupt noise of the gun firing startled her and caused her to flinch in anticipation. The movement of the gun did not seem to bother her. We had her use both ear plugs and muffs and this decreased the noise enough so she was able to concentrate on controlling the trigger press and keeping the sights aligned.

Some women shut their eyes as they press the trigger. They are thinking about how bad the recoil might be before it happens. If you close your eyes as you press the trigger, you can not see your sights and you will miss. You may blink just before your gun fires and not realize it because it happens so fast.

Muzzle flash

You may be startled by a flash of light or flame the first time you shoot in low light conditions. Muzzle flash is the last of the gun powder burning as the bullet leaves the muzzle. It is not visible during the day, but in low light it can be surprising if you have never seen it.

We had a female student who was greatly startled by the ball of flame that shot out from the muzzle. It was the first time she had ever fired in low light conditions. When she fired her first shot, she screamed that her gun was on fire! She thought the "fire" was coming right at her face. No one had ever explained to her how powder exiting the barrel continues to burn, creating a ball of fire at the end of the muzzle. We told her how this happens every time the gun is fired, but is not seen in daylight or under bright lights.

Recoil and accuracy

You have a job to do during recoil. Don't be overwhelmed mentally and physically. If you understand what is happening, you can learn to ignore the recoil and noise. You can fix what physically hurts you. If the noise is too much, use both foam plugs and ear muffs. If the gun hurts your hand, change the grips or change to a different gun. Learn to ignore the things that you cannot fix such as the push of energy against your hand. If you let the thoughts about recoil and noise get in your way, you will miss over and over again.

Do not let yourself react to the recoil before it happens. Stay focused on the sights and your smooth trigger press. Work past these speed bumps and be accurate!

Chapter 8

Safety

Your first concern when handling a firearm is safety. You must understand that guns are dangerous. It is unrealistic to demand some way to make firearms perfectly safe under all conditions. However you can learn to manage the risk.

Learning how to handle a gun safely requires a 100 percent commitment. We respect the power of a handgun and always use care and caution when handling one. Practicing firearms safety is not as difficult as you might think, but you must pay attention until the good habits described become second nature. There is no room for sloppy gunhandling!

It is important for you to understand that your ability to recite the following gun safety rules is only part of your responsibility. You need to develop a sense of awareness and focus on what you are doing every time you touch a gun.

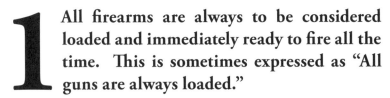

1 All firearms are always to be considered loaded and immediately ready to fire all the time. This is sometimes expressed as "All guns are always loaded."

The goal of this rule is for you to treat every gun you come in contact with as if it were loaded. We would like for you to be consistent in how you handle your gun and never allow yourself to ignore a safety rule because you think the gun is unloaded. Make it a habit to practice gun safety every time you touch a gun whether it is loaded or not.

You may observe people not handling their gun safely who say it is "safe" because the gun is unloaded, but that is when accidents happen. Unloading a gun does not give you permission to ignore safe gunhandling procedures. Do not allow others to risk your safety by saying "it's okay, the gun isn't loaded."

What is a loaded gun?

We define a loaded autoloader as one that has a round of ammunition in the chamber.

Revolvers are considered loaded if any of the chambers contains a round of ammunition.

What is an unloaded gun?

Autoloading handguns are considered unloaded when the magazine has been removed and there is no round of ammunition in the chamber.

Revolvers are considered unloaded when there are no rounds of ammunition in the chambers.

 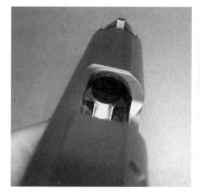

To determine if a handgun is loaded or not, you must visually and physically inspect the chamber. On an autoloading pistol, remove the magazine and lock the slide to the rear. Look inside for a round in the chamber and then use your finger to feel inside. Make it a habit to do both a visual and physical check as you might have to do this when it is dark or the light is dim.

Chapter 8: Safety

For a revolver, press the cylinder release lever and push the cylinder out away from the frame. Again you need to visually and physically inspect every chamber in the cylinder.

Refer to the Gunhandling Appendix for safe loading and unloading.

As a reminder, the muzzle is the end of the barrel where the bullet exits when the gun is fired.

2 The muzzle of your firearm must not, at any time, be allowed to point in an unsafe direction. This is sometimes stated as "Never let your muzzle cover anything that you are not willing to destroy."

A safe direction is defined as any direction that a gun is pointed where, if the gun is fired, the bullet will be stopped without damage or injury to yourself or other people. Handguns, unlike shotguns or rifles, have short barrels and can be held in one hand making it easier to swing the muzzle across your hand, arm, foot or other part of your body, or someone else's body. You must be focused on where the gun is pointed from the moment you pick it up until you put it down.

At a gun range, the backstop is a safe direction. This is the area where the targets are placed and it has been designed to safely absorb bullets fired from guns.

You are responsible for keeping the gun pointed in a safe direction. We encourage you to think about where you can safely point your gun when it is in your hand. Away from the range, a safe direction depends on your surroundings. In your home for example, you must be aware of the location of other people and pets. Could someone be in a room above, below or beside you?

Common wall construction of two-by-four inch lumber and sheetrock will not stop most handgun bullets. Items that can be used for a backstop are large appliances such as a refrigerator or heavy wooden furniture. Another safe direction might be a row of books or a filing cabinet filled with paper. Ceramic is another effective bullet stopper. Pointing your gun at a ceramic toilet bowl is a safe direction.

A Safe Direction® Academy Pad and Range Bag. These items contain Kevlar and are designed to contain a handgun round. They allow you to carry a safe direction with you.

Spatial relationships are an integral part of safe gunhandling. You must develop a specific awareness of where your gun is pointed. You must also learn to be conscious of where your trigger finger is and what it is doing.

As you are learning the fundamentals of shooting, it is up to you to keep your gun pointed in a safe direction. If you are working with an instructor or range officer, they can help watch where the gun is pointed. But if you are alone, the responsibility is yours. Remember, an unsafe direction includes any part of your body such as your hands, arms, legs or feet. The muzzle must not point in the direction of other people even for an instant!

> **Tip**
>
> Think of your gun as a light saber. A laser beam extends from the muzzle for as far as your eye can see. Anything that the light touches will be harmed. A common handgun bullet can travel over a mile.

Chapter 8: Safety

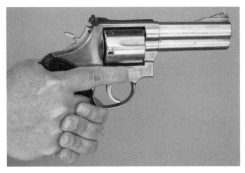 

Your trigger finger is the index finger of your strong hand.

3 **Your trigger finger must be in register against the frame and above the trigger guard until the sights are aligned on a target and the decision to fire has been made. This is sometimes expressed as "Keep your finger off the trigger until your sights are on target."**

Your trigger finger is *only* placed on the trigger when the gun is at eye level and your eye, rear sight, front sight and target are aligned *and* you have made the decision to fire. The most common reaction of a novice picking up a firearm is to immediately put her finger on the trigger. After all, that is what she has seen thousands of times on television programs and in movies. This is also the natural way most people pick up or grasp objects. For example, we wrap all of our fingers around a fork or toothbrush. This natural instinct must be overcome by mental focus and repetition.

4 **When you are pointing a gun at a target, you must be sure the target has been identified and that the area around and behind it is clear and safe to shoot at. This is also expressed as "Be sure of your target and what is beyond."**

On a range, targets are placed in front of a backstop designed to stop bullets. If you are shooting at a paper target, be aware that the bullet will pass right through the paper and into the designated backstop. It is your responsibility to make sure your bullet will be safely stopped.

> Most shooting ranges have rules regarding the types of target that can be used. Be aware that shooting at metal targets can cause part of the bullet to fly back toward you.

Safety equipment you must have

Eye and ear protection are designed to help prevent damage to soft tissue that is not easily repaired.

It is a good idea to make sure everyone who is on the range is wearing eye and ear protection even if they are not shooting. Your eyes can be damaged by a tiny sliver of metal, an ejected case or the hot gases produced by your gun or others shooting nearby. You also want to be protected from any fragments coming back from the target.

Vicki's safety glasses with a fragment of copper bullet jacket embedded in the lense.

Glasses that wrap around the side of your face provide the most protection. We strongly suggest that shooters wear a baseball-type hat or visor pulled low in order to keep ejected cases from falling between their eyes and glasses.

Safety glasses are available at gun shops, hardware stores and safety equipment supply stores. A good case will prevent them from being scratched.

Ear protection

Our ears can be damaged by the loud noise made when a gun fires. The intensity of sound is measured in decibels. We start to feel discomfort when we are

Chapter 8: Safety

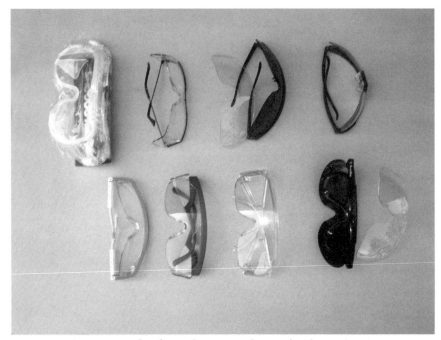

A variety of safety glasses with good side protection, including a prescription pair (lower right).

exposed to sounds greater than 85 decibels and pain when the noise reaches 120 decibels. A 22 caliber rifle will produce around 144 decibels while a 357 Magnum revolver produces about 172 decibels.

There are several options for hearing protection ranging from expandable foam inserts to earmuffs to custom in-the-ear electronic plugs. All of these work well to reduce the noise of a gunshot. Many women are sensitive to loud noises and may find it more comfortable to wear both foam inserts and earmuffs over them.

> **Technical tip**
>
> Under federal law, all hearing protection is marked with a noise reduction rating (NRR) with the maximum NRR being 35. There are variations, but in general, you should look for ear protection with a rating of NRR 21 or better.

Expandable foam ear plugs

Foam ear plugs are very inexpensive and are usually used once and thrown away.

Various ear protection plugs and muffs, included a customized molded set of plugs (upper right) and electronic muffs with amplifiers (lower right).

It is important to put them in correctly, because any gap will allow the sound of the gunshot to reach your ear canal. Start by compressing the plug into a small cylinder. You can do this by rolling the foam between your thumb and index finger or rolling it across the palm of your hand. Next insert the plug and gently hold it while the foam expands. If you have trouble inserting the plug, try pulling up on the top of your ear, as this helps to open the ear canal. Women tend to have smaller ear canals then men. If you have trouble inserting the compressed plug you might want to look for a smaller size.

Pre-molded ear plugs

You can also find pre-molded ear plugs. They are designed to be reused and are available in small, medium and large sizes. Some manufacturers make these ear plugs attached to one another with a string or sometimes on a flexible band that fits over your head. This allows you to remove the plugs and keep them hanging around your neck.

Chapter 8: Safety

Earmuffs

Muff-style hearing protectors are very convenient because they can be quickly put on or taken off. They need to fit snugly over your ears and safety glasses. Check to make sure the foam is still pliable enough to fit snugly over your safety glasses. A gap between the foam and your head will allow loud noise to reach your ear.

Several manufacturers offer electronic earmuffs. These have electronics that reduce noise at higher levels but allow you to hear people talking when the noise level is low. These are more expensive than other types of hearing protection.

Clothing

Autoloading handguns eject empty cases as they are fired. These cases are hot and can burn your skin if they are trapped behind your glasses or in your clothing. We encourage shooters to wear shirts that do not fall open at the neck. It is very difficult to remain focused on where your gun is pointed when a hot case falls down the front of your shirt, but you must control the gun and where it is pointing!

The arrow points to the cylinder gap between the forcing cone at the end of the barrel and the front of the cylinder.

Safety concerns for revolver shooters

Revolvers have a tiny gap between the cylinder and the barrel. Hot pressurized gases as well as tiny metal shavings fly out whenever the gun is fired. Never hold the gun here when it is fired. Your hand will be burned and possibly cut. Fingers are safe when using a proper grip.

Range safety rules

The rules on gun ranges can vary and it is important for you to first read the rules and ask questions before you start shooting. Ranges are usually designed for specific use and are designated as handgun, rifle or shotgun ranges. There may be restrictions on the caliber or type of ammunition you can use as well as the types of targets that are allowed.

Appendix

Gunhandling Skills

Your handgun is a part of your life. Practicing will make you comfortable and confident when you handle or shoot your gun. You will have an instructor to help you learn, but you are responsible for your own safety. You are the one who controls how you interact with the gun in your hand. Follow a routine and learn how to do each step until the procedure is as perfect as you can make it.

Become self reliant. It is easy to develop a crutch by avoiding responsibility. For example, if you always let someone else help you clean your gun or do it for you, you will never be comfortable doing it by yourself.

When we talk about safe gunhandling we mean:

You treat all guns as though they are loaded all the time.

You keep your finger off the trigger in the register position unless you are pointing your gun downrange and have decided to fire.

You keep the muzzle of your gun pointed in a safe direction any time it is in your hand.

Remember, the person most likely to be hurt if you fail to follow the firearms safety rules is you! You are the one in control of the gun in your hand. Do not let any part of your body pass in front of the muzzle. Never let the muzzle sweep past anyone else's body. Keep your finger off the trigger when it should not be there. You must be sure that you do not injure yourself or others or cause any property damage. Learn good gunhandling skills and use them all the time.

Competent gunhandling means you can safely handle your gun while doing the following:

- Unloading
- Loading
- Performing a chamber check
- Drawing from a holster

- Reholstering
- Reducing stoppages
- Taking your gun apart and reassembling it for cleaning purposes

In an academy, you will be taught a specific way to load, unload, draw and reholster your handgun. Our goal is to provide a basic foundation to build on. What we are describing are routines that are performed when there is no time limit. It is beyond the scope of this book to describe the tactical aspects of performing these gunhandling skills.

> **Tip**
> Having a reliable and simple core technique for these skills that you practice, along with a positive attitude, will improve your performance.

Having a consistent routine will help you to learn and practice safe gunhandling. If you always follow a routine, you eliminate the possibility of errors that can be harmful or dangerous. A routine prevents sloppy gunhandling and a casual attitude toward guns.

Here is an example of a simple routine to follow every time you are around firearms. Always determine where a safe direction is before you draw your gun or handle any gun for any reason.

Like most tools, guns are designed for right-handed people with average to large-sized hands and fingers. Women who are left-handed or have small hands and short fingers may have to modify how they handle their gun. Many left handers simply choose to do the techniques right-handed.

> These steps are sequential and must be followed in the proper order. If you change the order or skip a step, you will not end up with your gun in the condition you want it.

Unloading a semi-automatic or autoloading handgun

The following instructions are from the perspective of a right-handed woman.

Keep your gun pointed in a safe direction. Keep your finger off the trigger Never allow any part of your body to pass in front of the muzzle.

Appendix: Gunhandling Skills

Point your gun downrange. Grasp your gun in your right hand using the master grip with your trigger finger in the register position. This helps you control where the gun is pointed.

If your gun has a decocking lever, it must be pushed down to ensure the hammer is forward. If your gun has a manual safety that does not prevent the slide from moving, place it in the "on" position. If you are using a 1911-style or Browning handgun, placing the safety in the "on" position will prevent the slide from moving. In order to move the slide, place the lever in the "off" position.

Keeping your gun pointed downrange, turn your body 90 degrees to the right. Your gun will be close to your body, directly in front of your navel and pointed downrange. This position provides the best leverage for moving the slide. You can see the slide lock lever and the notch on the slide it goes into.

Using your right thumb, press the magazine release button and remove the magazine. You may have to rotate your hand a bit around the grip to reach the button. Learn to press the button without using your left hand. Allow the magazine to fall out into your left hand. If necessary, grasp the bottom of the magazine and pull it out while pressing the release button. Place the magazine in your pocket or waistband – not in your magazine pouch.

Rotate the gun so the ejection port is pointed down toward the ground. Make sure to continue to point the gun downrange.

With your left hand, come over the top of the slide (do not allow your hand to move in front of the muzzle) and grasp the slide behind the ejection port. Have the thumb laying parallel along the side of the slide. Be sure that your support elbow is not in front of the muzzle. Take care that your hand does not cover the ejection port.

Remove magazine with muzzle pointing downrange.

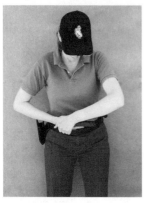 

Unloading Procedure: From low ready, turn your body 90 degrees to the target, remove the magazine, rack the slide to eject the round in the chamber, and lock the slide to the rear.

Rack the slide by rapidly pushing both of your hands together using your arms and shoulders to move the slide all the way to the rear. When the slide stops moving, let go with your left hand so the slide springs all the way forward again. This will eject the live round if one is in the chamber. Do not hold onto the slide as it moves forward.

Position your right hand so your thumb is underneath the slide lock lever. You might have to change your grip but remember to keep your trigger finger in the register position. Bring your left hand over the top of the slide, grasping

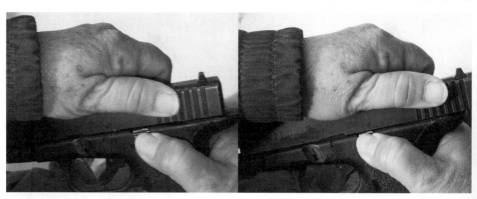

Locking the slide to the rear: Position strong thumb under the slide lock lever. Using the weak hand, move the slide to the rear until the slide lock lever slips into the notch in the slide, then release the slide with the notch holding it open.

Appendix: Gunhandling Skills

it behind the ejection port. Keep your left thumb parallel along the side of the slide. This position gives you the best leverage if you are learning to lock the slide back for the first time or have struggled and failed with this procedure before.

Push both hands together using your arms and shoulders while watching the notch that the slide lock lever pushes up into. When the notch is above the slide lock lever, push the lever upward to lock the slide back. The first few times you try this technique, it will probably feel awkward but with practice it becomes smooth.

Perform a visual and physical inspection of the chamber and magazine well. Use the little finger of your left hand to feel the opening of the chamber to determine that it is empty. The tip of your little finger will actually feel the opening of the chamber if it is empty or the base of the round of ammunition if one is still in the chamber. Push your finger down into the magazine well to make sure the magazine has been removed. This physical inspection allows you to determine the condition of your gun in low light or darkness.

> **Technical Tip**
>
> Once you have mastered this technique, locking the slide back even when the gun is at eye level and pointed downrange will become easier.

Loading an autoloading handgun

The following instructions are from the perspective of a right-handed woman.

Keep your gun pointed in a safe direction. Keep your finger off the trigger. Never allow any part of your body to pass in front of the muzzle.

Point your gun downrange. Grasp your gun in your right hand using the master grip with your trigger finger in the register position.

Turn your body 90 degrees to the right so you are holding your gun close to and directly in front of your navel. This position provides the best leverage for moving the slide.

With the slide locked to the rear, make sure the chamber and magazine well are empty. Insert a magazine using your left hand. Push the magazine all the way

If the slide is forward, insert the magazine, grasp the slide with your support hand and pull it all the way back and let it go. When the slide moves forward, it will load a round into the chamber. Tug on the bottom of the magazine to make sure it is secure.

into the magazine well using the heel of your left hand. You will hear a click as it locks into place. Tug on the magazine to make sure it is secure.

With your left hand, come over the top of the slide (do not allow your hand to move in front of the muzzle) and grasp the slide with your left hand placing it as far to the rear as possible.

Pull the slide all the way to the rear and let it go forward unassisted. Do not keep your left hand on the slide as it moves forward. The slide needs to slam forward. As the slide moves forward, it will strip the top round of ammunition out of the magazine and feed it into the chamber. The gun is now loaded.

If your gun has a decocking lever it must be depressed to lower the hammer. If your gun has a manual safety, it must be placed in the "on" position.

Keeping your finger in the register position, holster your gun.

Appendix: Gunhandling Skills

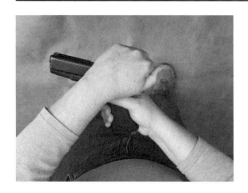
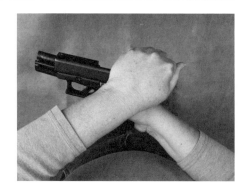
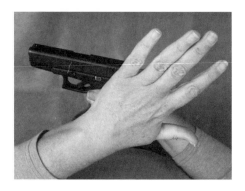

Remove the magazine while your gun remains in the holster. Replace the round of ammunition that was chambered when the slide moved forward. This topping off procedure insures you have a fully charged magazine.

Insert the magazine in the magazine well and push it up until it locks securely in place. The gun remains in your holster. Tug on the magazine to make sure it is secure in the magazine well.

To make sure none of your clothing is caught in your gun or holster, sweep your hand from back to front between the grip of your gun and your shirt.

> **Tip**
>
> As you become familiar with your gun and practice safe gunhandling, your fear will lessen and be replaced with a feeling of accomplishment and success.

Chamber check

A chamber check allows you to verify that a round of ammunition is in the chamber.

The following instructions are from the perspective of a right-handed woman.

Facing downrange, draw your gun and move it so the butt is in contact with your midriff.

If your gun has a manual safety that does not prevent the slide from moving, place it in the "on" position. If you are using a 1911-style or Browning handgun, placing the safety in the "on" position will prevent the slide from moving. In order to move the slide, place the lever in the "off" position.

Grasp your gun immediately forward of the trigger guard with your left hand by placing your thumb across the top of the slide and your other fingers underneath the frame. Do not allow your hand or fingers to cross in front of the muzzle.

Pull the gun backward until it is firmly braced against your midriff.

Rotate your right hand counter clockwise until your right thumb is under the tang of the frame and your fingers are hooked over the top of the slide. The further forward you can place your fingers, the better leverage you will have.

Clench your right hand so your fingers and thumb move toward one another. This will move the slide back just far enough for you to see inside the chamber.

Clamp the slide open by contracting your left hand. Now you can let go with your right hand and use your little finger to feel the round of ammunition. You need to be able to physically check this in case it is too dark to see.

Once you have confirmed there is a round of ammunition present, regain your master grip with your right hand. When you have control of the gun with your right hand, let go of your left hand and allow the slide to move forward and close.

Use the heel of your left hand to strike the back of the slide to make sure it is all the way forward.

If your gun has a manual safety, move it to the "on" position. If it has a decocker, be sure to decock.

Reholster your gun.

To make sure none of your clothing is caught in your gun or holster, sweep your hand from back to front between the grip of your gun and your shirt.

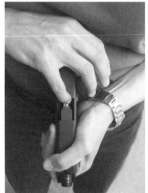

Chamber check instructions for the left-handed person

The following instructions are from the perspective of a left-handed woman.

Facing downrange, draw your gun and move it so the butt is in contact with your midriff.

If your gun has a manual safety that does not prevent the slide from moving, place it in the "on" position. If you are using a 1911-style or Browning handgun, placing the safety in the "on" position will prevent the slide from moving. In order to move the slide, place the lever in the "off" position.

Grasp your gun immediately forward of the trigger guard with your right hand by placing your thumb across the top of the slide and your other fingers underneath the frame. Do not allow your hand or fingers to cross in front of the muzzle.

Pull the gun backward until it is firmly braced against your midriff.

Rotate your left hand counter clockwise until your left thumb is under the tang of the frame and your fingers are hooked over the top of the slide. The further forward you can place your fingers, the better leverage you will have.

Clench your left hand so your fingers and thumb move toward one another. This will move the slide back just far enough for you to see inside the chamber.

Clamp the slide open by contracting your right hand. Now you can let go with your left hand and use your little finger to feel the round of ammunition. You need to be able to physically check in case it is too dark to see.

Once you have confirmed there is a round of ammunition present, regain your master grip with your left hand. When you have control of the gun with your left hand, let go of your right hand and allow the slide to move forward and close.

Use the heel of your right hand to strike the back of the slide to make sure it is all the way forward.

If your gun has a manual safety, move it to the "on" position. If it has a decocker, be sure to decock.

Reholster your gun.

Make sure none of your clothing is caught in your gun or holster, by sweeping your hand from back to front between the grip of your gun and your shirt.

Right-handed manipulation of a double action revolver

Unloading a double action revolver

Point the gun in a safe direction and keep your trigger finger in the register position. Make sure the hammer is forward. If the hammer is cocked, follow the instructions for lowering the hammer on page 93.

Hold the gun in your master grip with your trigger finger in the register position. Use your right thumb to work the cylinder release. The release works differently depending on the brand of revolver.

Swing the cylinder away from the frame using your left hand. Place your left hand so the cylinder lays between your thumb and index finger. Your index finger and middle fingers go through the open frame as the cylinder moves and remain on top of the cylinder. Your thumb wraps around the cylinder from underneath. This ensures that the cylinder can not close and allows you to hold

Appendix: Gunhandling Skills

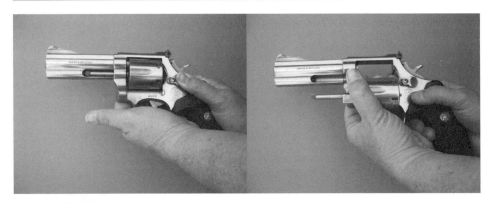

Unloading a revolver: Pointing in a safe direction, open and swing out the cylinder, rotate the gun to point up and hit the ejector rod with your weak hand.

the gun securely with your left hand.

Release your right hand. Point the muzzle up and allow the rounds of ammunition to fall out if they have not been fired. You will probably need to use the ejector rod to release rounds that have been fired. Keep the muzzle pointed up and, without allowing any part of your right hand to pass in front of the muzzle, position the heel of your hand over the top of the ejector rod and give it a swift smack. Do not try to catch the empty cases or rounds of

> **Technical tip**
>
> The cylinder release latch is pushed forward on Smith & Wessons, pulled back with Colts and pushed in with Ruger revolvers. Refer to your owners manual to determine how your cylinder release works.

ammunition. Let them fall to the ground.

Perform a visual and physical inspection of each chamber in the cylinder to make sure they are empty.

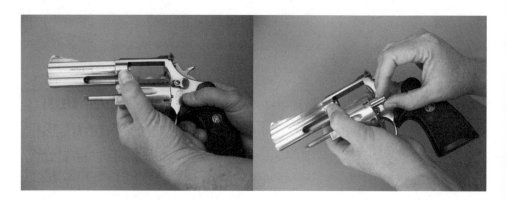

Loading a double action revolver

Open your cylinder following the directions above.

Keep your gun pointed in a safe direction and point the muzzle down. This allows gravity to help you load.

Use your right hand to pick up a round of ammunition and place it in an empty chamber. You can also use a speed loader. Loading manually, you can rotate the cylinder with your left thumb.

When all the chambers are full (or as many as you want), grip the gun with your right hand using the master grip. Use your left hand to push the cylinder

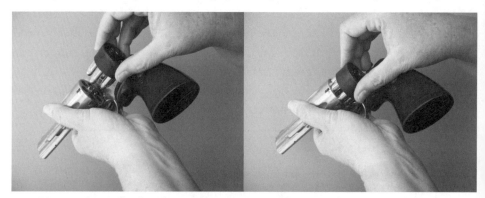

To use the Safariland speedloader, start the rounds into the chambers, then push it straight onto the back of the cylinder so that the spring releases the rounds. Remove the empty speedloader.

back into the frame until it locks in place. Do not slam the cylinder. When the cylinder is closed, you do not have to point the muzzle down. Rotate the cylinder in either direction until it locks into place and will not rotate further.

Reholster your revolver.

To make sure none of your clothing is caught in your gun or holster, sweep your hand from back to front between the grip of your gun and your shirt.

> **Technical tip**
>
> Speed loaders by HKS and Safariland make it possible to precisely and quickly load all chambers simultaneously. Their use is highly recommended.

Lowering the hammer of a double action revolver

If the hammer has been cocked and you do not intend to fire the gun immediately, the hammer must be lowered to its forward position. It is not safe to handle or carry a cocked double action revolver as it takes very little pressure to press the trigger and thus fire the gun.

You cannot open the cylinder of your revolver when the hammer is back.

Point your gun in a safe direction and grasp it with your right hand using the master grip. Your trigger finger is in the register position.

Place the thumb of your left hand between the cocked hammer and the back of the gun. This will prevent the hammer from falling all the way forward when pressure is applied to the trigger. If the hammer is not blocked, the gun will fire when the trigger is pressed (if the gun is loaded).

Keep your trigger finger in register until one thumb is on the hammer and the other thumb is under the hammer.

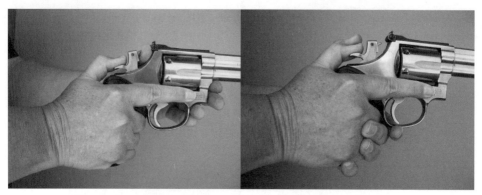

Press the trigger, then put your trigger finger back in register while you lower the hammer with your thumb.

Reach up and place your right thumb on the hammer spur. This allows you to control the hammer when it is released by the trigger.

When your left thumb is in place to block the trigger and your right thumb is on top of the hammer, press the trigger until you feel the hammer start to move forward. Immediately take your finger off the trigger and keep it in the register position along the side of the frame. When your finger is off the trigger, allow the hammer to move forward. At some point you will need to remove your left thumb from in front of the hammer so it can go all the way forward. Ease the hammer down all the way.

Once the hammer is all the way forward, you can use the cylinder release to unlock the cylinder and swing it out from the frame. Now you can inspect the chambers and either unload or load your gun.

Left-handed manipulation of a double action revolver

Unloading a double action revolver

Point your gun in a safe direction and keep your trigger finger in the register position. Make sure the hammer is forward. If the hammer is cocked, follow the instructions for lowering the hammer on page 96.

Hold the gun in your left hand and use your left index finger to work the cylinder release. The release works differently depending on the brand of revolver. You may have to change your grip by moving your hand down in order to reach the cylinder release. You can also use your right hand thumb by coming over the top of the frame.

Push the cylinder out away from the frame with your right thumb. Your thumb

Appendix: Gunhandling Skills

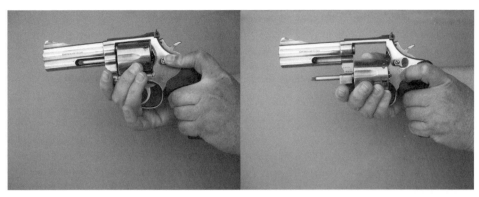

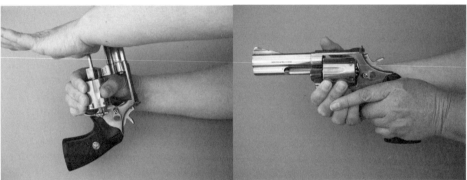

Using your index finger to open the cylinder (you may have to shift your master grip), rotate the cylinder out with your right hand and depress the ejector rod to eject brass.

will come through the frame and stay on top of the cylinder. The fingers on your right hand will wrap under the trigger guard to grasp the cylinder.

Release your left hand. Point the muzzle up and without allowing any part of your left hand to pass in front of the muzzle, use the palm of your left hand to hit the ejector rod. Allow the rounds of ammunition to fall out.

Loading a double action revolver

Open the cylinder following the directions above. Keep your gun pointed in a safe direction and point the muzzle down. This allows gravity to help you load.

Use your left hand to load the cylinder or use a speed loader. Rotate the cylinder with your right hand as needed.

When all the chambers are full (or as many as you want), grip the gun with your left hand using the master grip. Swing the cylinder closed with your right hand fingers without pinching your thumb. Do not slam the cylinder. When the cylinder is closed, you do not have to point the muzzle down. Rotate the cylinder in either direction until it locks into place and will not rotate further.

Reholster your revolver. To make sure none of your clothing is caught in your gun or holster, sweep your hand from back to front between the grip of your gun and your shirt.

Lowering the hammer of a double action revolver

If the hammer has been cocked and you do not intend to fire the gun immediately, the hammer must be lowered to its forward position. It is not safe to handle or carry a cocked double action revolver as it takes very little pressure to press the trigger and thus fire the gun.

You cannot open the cylinder of your revolver when the hammer is back.

Point your gun in a safe direction and grasp it with your left hand using the master grip. Your trigger finger is in the register position.

Place the thumb of your right hand between the cocked hammer and the back of the gun. This will prevent the hammer from falling all the way forward when pressure is applied to the trigger. If the hammer is not blocked, the gun will fire when the trigger is pressed (if the gun is loaded.)

Reach up and place your left thumb on the hammer spur. This allows you to control the hammer when it is released by the trigger.

When your right thumb is in place to block the trigger and your left thumb is on top of the hammer, press the trigger until you feel the hammer start to move forward. Immediately take your finger off the trigger and keep it in the register position along the side of the frame. When your finger is off the trigger, allow the hammer to move forward. At some point you will need to remove your right thumb from in front of the hammer so it can go all the way forward. Ease the hammer down all the way.

Once the hammer is all the way forward, you can use the cylinder release to unlock the cylinder and swing it out from the frame. Now you can inspect the chambers and either unload or load your gun.

Appendix: Gunhandling Skills

Drawing your handgun

Your handgun is not necessarily fired every time it is drawn. Sometimes you will draw your gun and fire immediately. Other times you will draw but refrain from firing. Do not get into the habit of firing your gun every time you draw.

If you are right-handed, your right hand is your strong hand. The right side of your body is your strong side and your left side is the support side. If you are left-handed, your left hand is the strong hand. Your left side is your strong side and your right is the support side.

Your strong hand is used to acquire your master grip with your trigger finger in the register position (flat along the frame above the trigger). Your support hand wraps around your strong hand.

Always be aware of where the muzzle is pointed and never allow it to point at any part of your body.

Face downrange and in your usual good stance, place your support hand flat against your stomach. This position keeps your hand from being in front of the muzzle. Learn to draw your gun using your strong hand only. Do not use your support hand to undo a snap or hold the holster down.

Index

Drop your strong hand to the butt of your handgun. Slide your hand forward until the web of your hand is snug against the tang.

If your holster has a thumb break snap, use your strong hand thumb to disengage the snap as your hand drops onto your gun.

Acquire your master grip while the gun is in the holster. Your trigger finger will be in the register position outside the holster. Make sure your wrist is locked and not angled up or down.

Clear

Using your strong hand, pull the gun up so the muzzle clears the top of the holster. Do not bend at the waist or roll your shoulder forward. Keep your torso and head still. Let your hands and arms move the gun.

Rock and lock

As soon as the muzzle clears the top of the holster, rock and lock your forearm and wrist. In other words, straighten your strong side wrist and rock you elbow downward. This will help you position your gun so the barrel is parallel with the ground. In this position, the gun can be fired using the strong hand only.

If your gun has a manual safety, it should be in the "on" position. Position your strong hand thumb on top of the lever. It is depressed to "off" after the gun is out of the holster and pointed at the target.

Unless you have decided to fire the gun immediately, your trigger finger is still in the register position.

Hands merge

From the rock and lock position, move the gun up toward eye level and into the firing position. As your gun moves forward, your support hand sweeps in from the side and joins the grip. It is critical that your hand does not cross in front of the muzzle when it comes into its support position on the grip.

Up strong to eye level

With both hands now joined on your gun's grip, bring it to eye level. Push the gun straight to the target. Your gun intersects the line between your eye and the target so your eye, the rear sight, front sight and the target are in a straight line.

If your gun has a manual safety, it is pushed to the "off" position. Learn to do this with your strong hand thumb.

Moving smoothly without unnecessary motion

Appendix: Gunhandling Skills

will bring your gun into a firing position quickly. Learn to move through the steps of the draw so there is no jerkiness.

> Learn to draw your gun without looking at your holster. Keep your head up and look straight at the target.

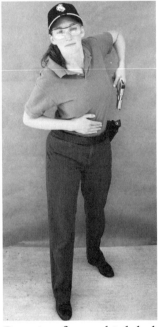

Drawing from a high holster causes a woman's body to contort more due to her short torso. Note the raised shoulder.

Technical tip

You may find there is little room between your holster and armpit. Do not bend at your waist to "create" more room. Instead, lift your shoulder and elbow straight up as high as necessary for the barrel to clear your holster. This minimizes your movement and is faster than bending from the waist.

(Left) Low ready from isosceles stance. (Right) Low ready from Weaver stance.

Low ready position

Once you have drawn your gun and brought it to eye level, if you do not shoot within a few seconds, assume the low ready position.

Drop your gun from eye level and point the muzzle down at a 45 degree angle. The muzzle will point at the ground a few feet in front of you. Keep your elbow and wrist angles the same. This allows you to bring the gun back to eye level quickly.

Your trigger finger returns to the register position as you bring the gun down. If your handgun has a manual safety, put it into the "on" position.

> **Technical tip**
>
> If your gun has a decocking lever and you have fired your gun, you must decock it before reholstering.

Reholstering

Learn to reholster using only your strong hand. Do not use your support hand to stabilize your holster or move a thumb strap.

Appendix: Gunhandling Skills

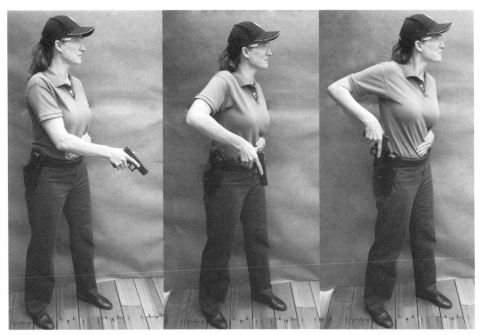

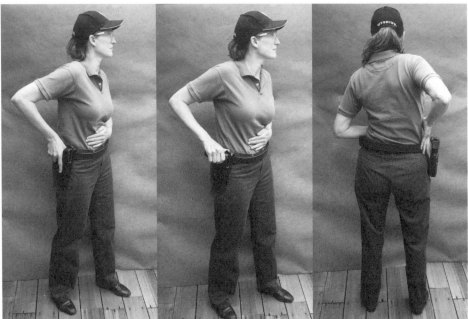

Steps of the reholster sequence.

With practice, you will be able to draw and reholster your gun safely without having to think about each step.

From the ready position:

Keep your trigger finger in the register position.

Remove your support hand from the grip and place it flat on your stomach.

Point the muzzle of the gun toward the ground. Do not allow the muzzle to point at your body or swing backward or forward as it is reholstered. Keep it pointed straight down.

Move your gun so it is behind your holster.

Move your gun forward, raising it to clear the holster until the muzzle is against the front edge of the opening of your holster.

Push your gun down into the holster as far as it will go.

Make sure none of your clothing is caught in your gun or holster by sweeping your hand from back to front between the grip of your gun and your shirt.

Simple stoppage reduction

If you experience a stoppage (the gun fails to fire when you press the trigger) keep your gun pointed in a safe direction.

Immediately hit the bottom of the magazine with your support hand.

Reach up and grab the slide and jerk it to the rear.

Reposition you support hand and attempt to fire again if that is what you want to do. This is also known as tap, rack, respond.

If this does not fix the problem, do not waste time trying it over and over. You will need to take further action by removing the magazine, working the slide vigorously several times and then reloading and attempting to fire if needed.

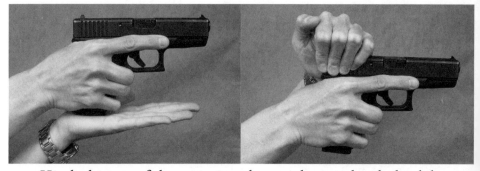

Hit the bottom of the magazine, then reach up and grab the slide.

Appendix: Gunhandling Skills

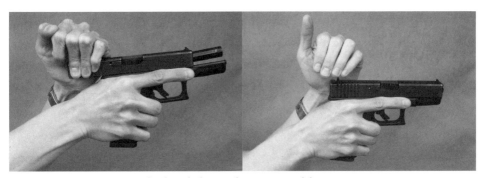

Jerk the slide to the rear and let it go.

Cleaning

It is beyond the scope of this book to provide detailed information on how to clean your handgun. Ideally you will have someone help you learn how to take your handgun apart, clean it and reassemble it. You may find it easier to learn by watching someone rather than trying to follow the words and pictures in your owner's manual.

When you are cleaning your gun, you may find that your hand is in front of the muzzle or the gun ends up pointed in an unsafe direction. We suggest that you try to set up your cleaning area so you can follow as many safety rules as possible.

> **Safety Tip**
>
> You must verify that your gun is unloaded before your start to clean it. Do both a visual and physical inspection of the chamber. Remove all ammunition from the area (it can be damaged by the chemicals used in cleaning.)

Identify your gun

The caliber and model of your handgun is stamped on the barrel or slide.

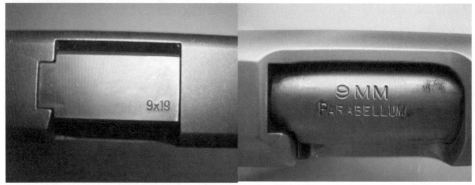

Autoloaders may have the ability to use barrels in different calibers, so the caliber designation is usually on the barrel, not the slide.

(Left) The caliber designation on the barrel of a revolver near the muzzle.

Taking your gun out of a case, bag or gun safe

When you arrive at the range, keep your gun in the case until you are at the firing line. When you take your gun out of its case, keep it pointed downrange. Remember to keep it pointed downrange while you load or unload it.

How do I hand my gun to another person?

The easiest way is to unload the gun. For an autoloader, remove the magazine, lock the slide to the rear and visually and physically inspect the chamber. For a revolver, press the cylinder release and push the cylinder away from the frame. Visually and physically inspect each chamber in the cylinder.

Lay the gun down and allow the other person to pick it up. It is their responsibility to check the condition of the gun. Remember to handle all guns as though they are loaded—finger off the trigger in the register position and the muzzle always pointed in a safe direction.

Appendix: Gunhandling Skills

If you cannot put the gun down, remove the magazine, unload the gun and leave the slide locked to the rear. For the revolver, press the cylinder release and push the cylinder out away from the gun. Inspect to make sure there are no rounds of ammunition in the cylinder. Hold the gun so the person taking it can put their hand on the grip. Make sure the person taking the gun has control of it before you let go so the gun will not fall to the ground.

Glossary

Accuracy - Hitting the target where you intend to hit it.

Ammunition - Handgun ammunition (also called a round of ammunition or cartridge) is made from several components: a metal case, a primer, a bullet and gunpowder.

Hollowpoint ammunition (from the left) in 9mm, 38 Special, 357 Magnum, 40S&W, 357 Sig, 45 ACP and 400 Cor-Bon®.

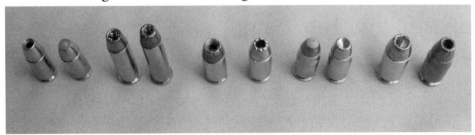

Autoloader - A handgun that automatically reloads after each round is fired (also known as a semi-automatic). You must press the trigger for every shot. A fully automatic handgun or machine gun will continue to fire as long as the trigger is held down and there is ammunition.

There are basically two types of handguns, the revolver and the autoloading or semi-automatic pistol. We use the terms autoloader and semiauto

interchangeably.

Backstrap - The rear surface of the grip; the back of the gun's handle.

Barrel - Metal tube down which the bullet travels from the chamber to the muzzle. Handgun barrels have spiral grooves inside to impart a spin to the bullet.

From the top, disassembled slide, recoil spring, barrel, frame and magazine from a SIG P239 semiauto pistol.

Bullet - The metal projectile fitted inside the cartridge case. The bullet separates from the case when the gun fires and is pushed out the barrel and downrange.

Cartridge - A round of ammunition, consisting of a case, primer, gunpowder and bullet.

Cartridge case - The metal case containing the primer, bullet and gunpowder.

Catching the link, or **trigger reset** for multiple shots - When you hold the trigger to the rear after the gun fires, you will be able to catch the link when you take your next shot by easing the trigger forward just enough to reengage the sear. You will hear or feel a click when this happens.

Clutter - Unhelpful thoughts that distract you from being mentally focused and in control of your body.

Glossary

Cylinder - The round metal part of a revolver with holes called chambers bored through it to hold cartridges.

Cylinder gap - The space between the front of the cylinder and the rear end of the barrel. When a revolver fires, the bullet has to cross this gap, allowing hot gas to escape out the side of the gap. When firing, it is important to keep your fingers behind the front of the cylinder to avoid these gases.

Cylinder release latch (left) and revolver cylinder, which swings out from the frame after pushing the cylinder release latch, just behind the cylinder. (Below Right) Cylinder gap.

Cylinder release - The lever on the left side of a revolver, used to open the cylinder.

Decocking lever - A lever used to decock (lower) the hammer on some semiautos without firing the gun.

Double-action-only handgun - A handgun in which pressing the trigger is the only way to cock and release the hammer or striker. The trigger pull is the same for every shot.

Decocking lever (arrow) on a Sig P239. Note cocked hammer before pushing down on decocking lever. It is spring activated. Other lever is a slide lock.

109

Decocking lever on a S&W 3913LS. Note cocked hammer with lever up. The lever stays down, deactivating the trigger, and must be pushed up to fire the gun.

Double action revolver - A double action revolver can be fired in either single or double action mode. The single action mode is achieved by cocking the hammer with your thumb. Once you apply a slight pressure to the trigger, the gun will fire.

In the double action mode, the hammer is forward and all you do is press the trigger. It will take several pounds of pressure because you are rotating the cylinder and cocking the hammer. The trigger pull is heavy.

Double action semiauto - A pistol that has the hammer down, so pressing the trigger both cocks and drops the hammer.

Dry fire - Pulling the trigger on an empty firearm for practice. Obey the safety rules even though the gun is empty!

Ear protection - Plugs fit into the ear canal to dampen noise. Muffs cover your entire ear to block loud noise.

Various ear protection plugs and muffs, including a customized molded set of plugs (upper right) and electronic muffs with amplifiers (lower right).

Glossary

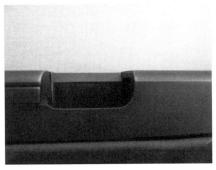

Ejection port on the right side of the slide of a semiauto pistol. The outside of the extractor is visible at the left.

Ejection port - The opening in the slide of an autoloading handgun through which the empty case is ejected from the gun after it fires.

Ejector - The fixed part at the back of the ejection port that flings the cartridge case out of the gun after it is extracted from the chamber.

Extractor - The device on the slide of an autoloading handgun that grabs the edge of the cartridge case and pulls it from the chamber after the gun has fired.

Finger in register - Your trigger finger is placed flat along the frame above the trigger and trigger guard of your gun. There are two places for your trigger finger when you are holding your gun: in the register position when you are not shooting, or on the trigger when your sights are on the target and you have

(Above) Finger in register on a revolver and semiauto.

(Left) Finger on the trigger on a semiauto.

made the decision to fire your gun.

Finger on the trigger - The position of your finger when the sights are on target and the decision to fire has been made.

Firearm safety - The proper handling of a gun to ensure there is no unintended personal injury or destruction of property.

Firearm safety rules - The four universal rules for safe gunhandling. See chapter 8.

Focus - The ability to mentally concentrate on what your body is doing. For accurate shooting you need to focus your eye to clearly see the front sight and confirm that it is aligned while you press the trigger. Clear your mind of clutter and stay in control of what your body is doing.

From the top, the slide, recoil spring, barrel, frame (with grips) and magazine of a Sig P239 semiauto pistol.

Below, grip panels removed from a semiauto, and a revolver with replacement grip panels installed.

Frame - The solid part of your handgun to which all other parts are attached.

Grip - The part of the gun you hold with your firing hand. Grip is also used to describe how you place your hands on your gun.

Grips or **grip panels** - Removable or changeable coverings for the grip of your gun.

Glossary

(Upper left) The barrel of a Glock 19 shows "9x19" to designate 9mm.

(Upper right) The barrel of an S&W 3913 is also 9mm.

(Left) An S&W revolver has the caliber marked on its barrel.

Gun - A machine used to launch a bullet.

Gun fit - The size of a handgun in relation to the size of your hand determines how well the gun fits. A gun that fits allows you to easily acquire a proper grip and trigger finger placement.

Identify your gun - Your handgun has markings that describe the brand, model and caliber. This information can be found on the slide or barrel of an autoloader and on the barrel of a revolver.

Isometric muscle tension - One set of muscles pulling and one set of muscles pushing against one another.

Isosceles stance - A stance with your body directly facing the target and both arms nearly straight but not locked.

Isosceles stance seen from the right side.

Launch Platform - A routine that helps you improve your accuracy.

Limp wrist - The wrist is at an angle and not locked. This position does not provide support for your gun when it fires. If you are shooting an autoloading handgun, the slide may not function properly and the gun may fail to eject the empty case or feed a new round of ammunition into the chamber.

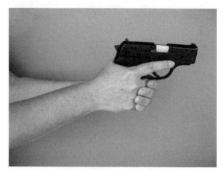

      Limp Wrist   Locked Wrist

Loaded gun - If a handgun has a round of ammunition in the chamber, it is considered loaded.

     Loaded Revolver   Loaded Semiauto

Locked wrist - The wrist joint is locked and the forearm is parallel to the ground. This position provides good support for your handgun. Your wrist can be locked even if your hand is rotated on the grip.

Magazine - A metal container inserted into the magazine well of an autoloading handgun that holds the rounds of ammunition in position until they are loaded into the chamber.

Magazine release - A button or lever that unlocks the magazine from the magazine well of an autoloading handgun and allows it to be removed.

Glossary

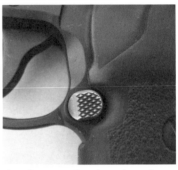

Magazines, some with witness holes. Note the thickness of the double-stack magazine on the right. In it cartridges are staggered in two columns. (Right) Magazine release button.

Manipulating the slide - Manually moving the slide of an autoloading handgun backwards and forwards.

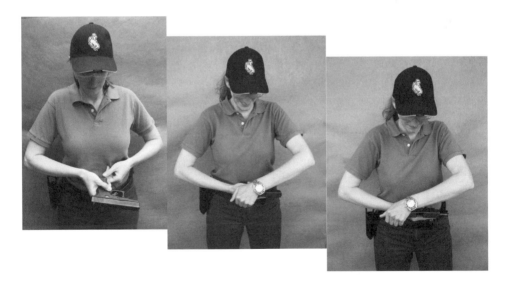

Manipulating the slide. Keep the muzzle pointed downrange and away from your elbow.

Master grip - The ideal position of your hands on the grip of your gun.

Muzzle - The end of the barrel where the bullet exits.

Muzzle awareness - Knowing where the muzzle is pointed when the gun is in your hand.

Range - An area designed for shooting firearms so the bullets are absorbed or contained without causing harm or damage.

Recoil - The energy felt by the shooter when the gun fires.

(Left) The muzzle of a Glock 19.

(Right) Vicki fires an S&W 500 Magnum, which shows serious muzzle flip on recoil.

Register position - The position of your trigger finger when you are not firing your gun. Your finger is placed flat against the frame above the trigger and trigger guard.

Glossary

Risk - Stepping out of your comfort zone to perform a task that can result in success or failure.

Round - Another name for a cartridge.

Safe direction - A back stop that will contain, absorb or stop bullets.

Safe Direction® product - A self contained portable back stop using Kevlar.

A Safe Direction® Academy Pad and Range Bag.

Safe guns and **dangerous guns** - There are no safe guns. All guns should be treated as loaded and dangerous. Some guns such as the 1911 have a manual safety you must manipulate. The Glock pistols have a passive safety on the trigger that is used every time you press the trigger. All handguns have internal safety mechanisms that function without input from the shooter.

A variety of glasses with good side protection, include a prescription pair.

Safety glasses - Glasses with polymer or glass lenses that are designed to be resistant to impact. Always a good idea.

Safety rules - Four universal rules for safe gunhandling. See chapter 8.

Self-decocking autoloader - The trigger of this kind of autoloader follows the slide forward and does not remain cocked. The trigger pull is the same for every shot. For example, the Glock, the Sig DAK trigger or the H&K LEM trigger.

Sight alignment - When the gun is at eye level, you look through the rear sight and align the front sight so the top of the front sight is level with the top of the rear sight. In other words, you could draw a straight line across the tops of the rear and front sights. The front sight is centered within the rear sight with equal amounts of light on both sides.

Sight picture - What you see when you look at a target and there is a straight line between your eye and the target. You bring your gun to eye level and intersect this line with the rear and front sights properly aligned.

Sight alignment.

Sight picture.

Sights, front and rear - The devices on the top of the slide or barrel that allow your eye to aim the gun at the point on the target where you wish to have the bullet hit.

Single action autoloader - The trigger only performs one function; it releases the hammer or striker. The trigger pull is short and light and is the same for every shot. These guns have a manual safety that locks the slide in place when the hammer is cocked. The safety must be removed before the gun will fire.

Slide - The slide sits on top of the frame and surrounds the barrel of an autoloading handgun. This part moves backwards and forwards when the gun fires. The slide can be manually locked to the rear so you can inspect the chamber and magazine well. When the gun fires, the slide moves backwards and opens the

Glossary

ejection port. The empty case is pulled out and ejected as the slide moves back. The slide then moves forward and picks up a round of ammunition from the top of the magazine and loads it into the chamber.

Slide lock or release lever - The device located on the left side of the frame that can be pushed up to lock the slide open when it is pulled to the rear. Pressing down on the lever will release the slide letting it move forward.

A Glock 19 with slide locked to the rear by the slide lock lever in the bottom center of the slide. Slide locks on other guns will have different shapes and be in different positions.

From the top, disassembled slide, recoil spring, barrel, frame and magazine from a SIG P239 semiauto pistol.

Spatial relationship - This is your ability to picture objects, their shape, position, proportion and their relationship to one another in your mind's eye. Spatial relationship is used to accurately hit your target by understanding how your eye, rear and front sight and the target are aligned.

Strong hand - If you are right-handed, your right hand is your strong hand. If you are left-handed, your left hand is your strong hand.

Support hand - If you are right-handed, your left hand is your support hand. If you are left-handed, your right hand is your support hand.

Tang - The backward curve at the top of the grip below the slide.

The thumbs up grip. This grip will not interfere with the slide operation. It allows more of the support hand to be in contact with the grip of the gun.

Thumbs up grip - Your strong and support thumbs are pointed up as you grip your autoloading gun. This thumb position keeps your support hand high on the grip and will help you control your gun.

Trigger - The trigger is where you place your trigger finger when you have made the decision to fire your gun. When the trigger is pressed all the way back, the hammer is released starting the chain of events that causes the gun to fire.

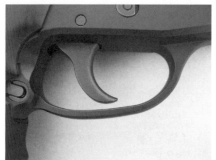 

(Left) Sig trigger in forward (double-action) position. (Right) Glock trigger showing the distinctive Glock passive safety on the lower face.

Your trigger finger is the index finger of your strong hand. Do not place the index finger of the support hand on the front of the trigger guard.

Glossary

Trigger control - Pressing the trigger using a smooth steady pressure while maintaining the alignment of the rear and front sights to ensure an accurate hit on the target.

Trigger face - The flat front portion of the trigger where the first pad of your trigger finger (index finger) is placed when firing the gun.

Trigger finger - The index finger of your strong hand. If you switch your gun to a master grip in your support hand, the index finger of your support hand will be your trigger finger.

Trigger finger fatigue - Fatigue happens when the muscles in the hand and finger get tired and no longer have enough strenght to press the trigger.

Trigger finger placement - The exact position where you will place your finger on the face of the trigger depends on the amount of pressure it takes to move the trigger and the distance the trigger must move. If your trigger only takes a few pounds of pressure to move, center the pad of your finger on the trigger about half way between the tip of your finger and the first joint. If the trigger on your handgun is heavier, you will need more leverage to press it back. Push the tip of your finger across the trigger until the face of the trigger presses into the first joint.

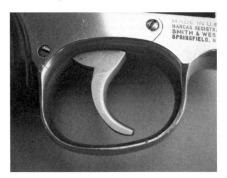 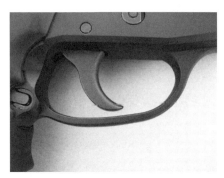

Trigger guards for a revolver and a semiauto,
both in double action (forward) position.

Trigger guard - A part of the frame that starts in front of the trigger and curves around below the trigger to meet the frame again behind the trigger.

Unloaded gun - A handgun that does not have a round of ammunition in the chamber.

 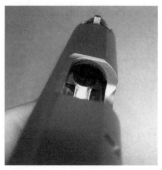

(Left) An unloaded revolver showing empty chambers in the cylinder.

(Right) An unloaded semiauto chamber seen through the ejection port.

Weaver stance - An isometric stance in which the body is turned at a 45 degree angle, with the strong side back, the strong arm almost straight and the weak elbow pointing down at the ground. The strong arm pushes forward and the weak arm pulls back.

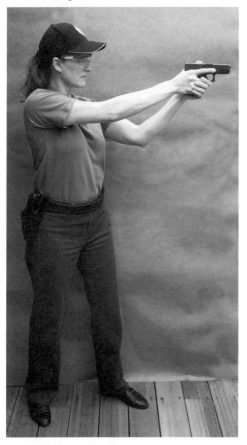

Weaver stance demonstrated for a right-handed shooter. Note left elbow pointed down and right elbow slightly flexed.

Index

A

Accuracy 2, 5, 13, 17, 27, 48, 59, 70, 107
Accurate shot 1, 2
All guns are always loaded 71
Ammunition 107
Anticipation of recoil 63

B

Backstrap 19

C

Catching the link 59
Chamber check 88
Cleaning 103
Clear 97
Confirm sight alignment 30, 32, 33, 37, 48, 56, 60
Consistently missing 37
Continuous trigger contact 48, 59

D

Decocking lever 27
Decocking lever 83, 100, 109
Drawing 96
Dry fire 50, 60
Dry fire drill 61

E

Earmuffs 78
Ear plugs 77
Ear protection 76
Exercise, strength 52
Exercise, trigger control 51
Exercise, trigger finger control 51
Eye level 5, 10, 13, 29, 98
Eye protection 76

F

Felt recoil 64
Finger in register 75, 111

Finger on the trigger 112
Flinching 63
Focus 31, 56, 112
Focus, mental 2, 42, 75, 112
Front sight 29, 30, 32, 38, 41, 55

G

Grip 17
Grip covers 17, 67
Grip of the gun 17
Grip on the gun 17
Gunhandling skills 81

H

Hand placement 27
Hand size 66, 67
Hands merge 98
Hearing range 63
High holster 99

I

Identify your gun 103
Index 97
Isosceles stance 9

J

Jerking 63

L

Launch Platform 5, 55
Left-handed 14, 94
Limp wrist 25
Loaded gun 72
Loading 85
Loading revolver 92
Location of the sights 29
Locked wrist 25
Locking slide to the rear 84
Lowering the hammer 93
Low ready 12, 100

M

Machine, handgun as ix, 113
Magazine 114

Index

Magazine release 115
Managing recoil 64
Manipulating the slide 116
Master Grip, Ideal 18
Master Grip, Modified 20
Missing 57
Moving target 59
Muzzle flash 69
Muzzle flip 27, 64

N

Night sights 37
Noise 68

P

Press 2, 18, 23, 29, 33, 41, 46, 47, 52, 55, 59

Q

Qualification 2

R

Range safety rules 79
Rear sight 29, 34, 37
Recoil 63
Recoil and accuracy 70
Recoil and speed 66
Reholstering 100
Revolver grip 26
Revolver safety 79
Risk 1
Rock and lock 98

S

Safe direction 73
Safety 71
Safety equipment 76
Safety glasses 76
Sear 48, 59
Sensitive ears 69
Sight alignment 29
Sight picture 118
Size and shape of hand 66
Small hands 23
Speed loaders 93

Squeeze 47, 51, 58
Stance 5
Stoppage reduction 102
Strength 11, 13
Strong elbow 8
Strong hand 97
Strong side 6
Support elbow 8, 15
Support hand 22
Support side 6, 97

T

Tang 19, 24, 88, 120
Target 75
Tennis elbow 68
Thumbs-up grip 19, 65
Thumbs up 14, 23, 120
Trajectory ix, 37
Trigger control 41
Trigger face 21, 121
Trigger finger 75
Trigger finger placement 42
Trigger guard 19, 26, 122
Trigger press ix, 18, 23, 29, 33, 41, 47
Trigger reset 48, 59, 108
Trigger weights 43
Types of sights 37
Types of triggers 53

U

Unloaded gun 72
Unloading 82
Unloading revolver 90
Up strong to eye level 98

W

Weaver stance 6

Resources

Safe Direction® Range Bag and Academy Pad

Safe Direction
PO Box 1249
Addison IL 60101-1249
Phone 877-357-4570
Illinois 630-628-3178
Fax 630-543-0524

For other products recommended by John and Vicki Farnam, and for the latest news from DTI Publications, Inc, see our web page, **www.dtipubs.com** and the **Resources** page near the bottom of the left column.

Defense Training International, Inc.

For information on training by John and Vicki Farnam, see their web page, **www.defense-training.com** or contact them by phone at 970-482-2520.

Notes

Farnam Method of Defensive Shotgun and Rifle Shooting

by John S Farnam

The Farnam Method of Defensive Shotgun and Rifle Shooting
by John S. Farnam

John Farnam's years of experience in the military as well as law enforcement have allowed him to gain first hand knowledge of what works most reliably in real-life lethal force confrontations. This book provides information regarding the types of defensive shotguns and rifles as well as the tactics for using them.

208 pages, 1997, List Price: $19.95

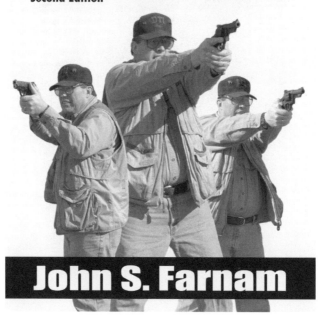

The Farnam Method of Defensive Handgunning, Second Edition
by John S. Farnam

This is the most comprehensive book about the defensive use of handguns in your home and daily life. John Farnam presents the most up-to-date information regarding the types of defensive handguns, ammunition and the tactics for using them effectively. How to adopt the "Stealth Existence" to avoid confrontations. Newly revised and expanded.

272 pages, 2005, List Price: $25.00

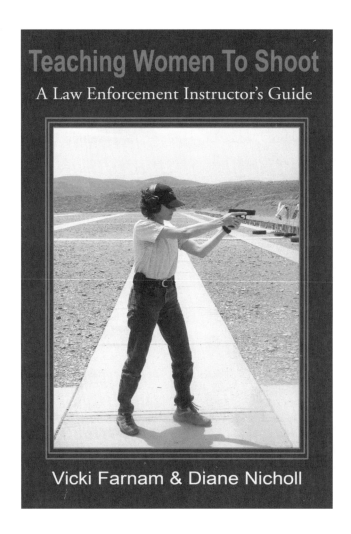

Teaching Women To Shoot: A Law Enforcement Instructor's Guide
by Vicki Farnam and Diane Nicholl

This book shows what problems many women have on the range, explains why the problems occur and shows instructors how to solve these problems. The authors share how they teach women the fundamentals of shooting.

136 pages, 2002, List Price: $19.95

DTI Publications, Inc
PO Box 18746
Boulder, CO 80308-1746

www.dtipubs.com

Books available from DTI Publications Inc

The Farnam Method of Defensive Shotgun and Rifle Shooting
by John S. Farnam, 1998

The Farnam Method of Defensive Handgunning (Second Edition)
by John S. Farnam, 2005

Teaching Women To Shoot: A Law Enforcement Instructor's Guide
by Vicki Farnam and Diane Nicholl, 2002

Women Learning To Shoot: A Guide for Law Enforcement Officers
by Diane Nicholl and Vicki Farnam, 2006

DTI Quips, Volume One (1998-2002)
by John S. Farnam, 2006

DTI Publications, Inc
PO Box 18746
Boulder, CO 80308-1746

Find us on the web at: **www.dtipubs.com**